I0820549

THE ETHIOPIANS

LOST CIVILIZATIONS

The books in this series explore the rise and fall of the great civilizations and peoples of the ancient world. Each book considers not only their history but their art, culture and lasting legacy and asks why they remain important and relevant in our world today.

Already published:

The Assyrians Paul Collins
The Aztecs Frances F. Berdan
The Barbarians Peter Bogucki
Egypt Christina Riggs
The Ethiopians Steven Kaplan
The Etruscans Lucy Shipley
The Goths David M. Gwynn
The Greeks Philip Matyszak
The Hittites Damien Stone
The Inca Kevin Lane
The Indus Andrew Robinson
The Maya Megan E. O'Neil
The Minoans Ellen Adams
Nubia Sarah M. Schellinger
The Persians Geoffrey Parker and Brenda Parker
The Phoenicians Vadim S. Jigoulov
The Sumerians Paul Collins
The Three Kingdoms of Korea Richard D. McBride II

THE ETHIOPIANS

LOST CIVILIZATIONS

STEVEN KAPLAN

REAKTION BOOKS

In memory of my sister Judy Sakowitz

For my sister Eva Kaplan

Published by Reaktion Books Ltd
2–4 Sebastian Street
London EC1V 0HE, UK
www.reaktionbooks.co.uk

First published 2025

EU GPSR Authorised Representative
Logos Europe, 9 rue Nicolas Poussin, 17000, La Rochelle, France
email: contact@logoseurope.eu

Printed and bound in India by Replika Press Pvt. Ltd

A catalogue record for this book is available from the British Library

ISBN 978 1 83639 102 9

CONTENTS

Chronology

3.2 million years ago — Lucy or *Dinkinesh*

c. 970–931 BCE — King Solomon's rule in ancient Israel

800–360 BCE — Pre-Aksumite Period

c. 700 BCE — Temple in Yəḥa

360–80 BCE — Proto-Aksumite Period

80 BCE–160 CE — Early Aksumite Period

c. 50 CE — Composition of the *Periplus of the Red Sea*

160–380 — Classic Aksumite Period

c. 200–270 — First Aksumite occupation of Ḥimyar

c. 330–80? — Reign of ʿEzana

c. 340 — Conversion of ʿEzana

380–580 — Middle Aksumite Period

c. 517–33 — Reign of Kaleb

518	Kaleb occupies Ḥimyar
522	Massacre of Christians at Nağrān
525	Kaleb's invasion of Ḥimyar and defeat of Dhū Nuwās
527–65?	Abraha in power in Ḥimyar
548	Conference at Mārib
c. 570	Traditional date of the birth of Muhammed
580–825	Late Aksumite Period
613 or 615	First *hiğra* (migration/separation)
825–	Post-Aksumite Period
896	Emergence of the Sultanate of Šawa
1137?–1270	The Zag^{w}e Period
Late 12th–early 13th century	Reign of Lalibäla
1270–85	Reign of Yəkunno Amlak
1285	Emergence of the Sultanate of Ifat
1314–44	Reign of ʿAmdä Ṣəyon
1344–72	Reign of Säyfä Arʿad
1348–88	Metropolitan Abunä Sälama II, 'the Translator'

1380–1412	Dawit II
1413–30	Reign of Yəsḥaq
1415	Emergence of the Sultanate of Adal
1434–68	Reign of Zär'a Ya'qob
1441	First European mention of the Oromo
1468–78	Reign of Bä'edä Maryam
1478–95	Reign of Əskəndər
1508–40	Reign of Ləbnä Dəngəl
1529	Troops of Gragn invade Ethiopia
1543	Troops of Galawdewos aided by Portuguese defeat and kill Gragn
1557	Ottoman capture of Massawa
1593	Bahrey's composition of *The History of the Galla*
1632–1769	Gondärine Period
1632–67	Reign of Fasilädäs
1635	Foundation of Gondär by Fasalädäs
1769–1855	Zämänä mäsafənt (Era of the Judges/Princes)
1784–1853	Yäǧǧu (Oromo) dynasty in power

1855	Kaśa becomes Tewodros II
1886	Mənəlik II establishes Addis Ababa
1889	Death of Yoḥannes IV
2 May 1889	Mənəlik II (acting emperor) and Italians sign Treaty of Wuchale
1 March 1896	Troops of Mənəlik II defeat the Italians in the Battle of Adwa
3 April 1930	Ras Täfari elevated to the throne as Haile Selassie I
1930s	Emergence of the Rastafari movement
3 October 1935	Italian invasion of Ethiopia
2 May 1936	Haile Selassie I flees Addis Ababa
9 May 1936	Italy annexes Ethiopia (Abyssinia)
5 May 1941	Haile Selassie I re-enters Addis Ababa
December 1950	UN resolution establishes Ethiopian–Eritrean Federation
13–16 December 1960	Failed coup by members of the Imperial Bodyguard and military
14 November 1962	Annexation of Eritrea
25 May 1963	Establishment of the Organization of African Unity in Addis Ababa

1973	Famine in Wällo
28 June 1974	Derg (Marxist Military Committee) established
12 September 1974	Derg deposes Emperor Haile Selassie
March 1975	Abolition of monarchy and establishment of Marxist–Leninist government
3 February 1977	Elevation of Mengistu Haile Mariam
May 1991	Derg is toppled by a combination of forces
1993	Eritrean independence
May 1998–June 2000	Badme War (Ethiopia and Eritrea)
27 March 2010	Launch of Ethiopian Academy of Sciences
11 October 2019	Prime Minister Abiy Ahmed awarded Nobel Peace Prize
November 2020	Conflict between central government and Təgray

Prologue

> Ethiopia shall soon stretch her hands out to God.
>
> PSALM 68:31

> Zeus went yesterday to Ocean to a feast with the blameless Ethiopians, and all the gods followed.
>
> HOMER, *Iliad*, 1.423

> I can't see the point in learning to solve useless problems, or subtracting turnips from turnips, or knowing where Ethiopia is or how to spell February.
>
> NORMAN JUSTER, *The Phantom Tollbooth*[1]

For many Western readers Ethiopia calls to mind two contradictory images: famine and food. On the one hand, the name conjures up images of war, starving refugees, conflict and want. On the other, it seems as if almost every major city in Europe and North America has at least one and usually several Ethiopian restaurants with evocative names like Red Sea, Blue Nile, Sheba, Lalibala or Aksum and (to quote *The Simpsons*) 'Haile Delicious' food![2] As I discuss below, behind these names and these images there lies the story of an ancient nation, home to numerous peoples, languages and religions.

Ethiopia is in what is commonly called the 'Horn of Africa', a promontory shaped like a rhinoceros horn which juts out into the

Axum (Aksum) Ethiopian Restaurant, Washington, DC.

Arabian Sea and the Indian Ocean. Within the Horn of Africa are several countries: Sudan, South Sudan, Kenya, Somalia, Djibouti and, of course, Ethiopia and Eritrea.

Over the course of centuries its political map has been repeatedly redrawn, mainly through the initiatives of local peoples, but more recently via colonial fiat or superpower interventions. Numerous bloody wars have resulted. Even as I write these words, conflicts rage within and between several of the region's states. Located at the intersection of Africa and the Middle East (West Asia), with sea routes that link East Africa, India and East Asia, this region has since time immemorial been the meeting place of cultures, faiths and the material products of long-distance trade.[3] Since the beginning of the Common Era, goods and ideas from both the Mediterranean Sea and the Indian Ocean flowed through its harbours. In some periods products from as far away as China were imported.

Several scholars, most notably the Cambridge University sociologist Jack Goody, have seen Ethiopia as 'geographically inside the continent of Africa, but culturally outside'.[4] Or, to borrow a phrase from a recent study of Blackness in Greek antiquity, '*in* Africa but not *of* Africa'.[5] Because the Ethiopians used the plough, had a written language, adopted Christianity and utilized a 'feudal' system of land tenure, Ethiopia would seem to be an excellent case for comparison with medieval Europe. Indeed, it has become increasingly common for there to be panels on Ethiopia at conferences of medieval studies as the idea of a 'Global Middle Ages' develops and expands.[6]

And yet, for many people, Ethiopia is the *African* country par excellence. Mentioned at least 45 times in most English translations of the Hebrew Bible, with the large-scale arrival of European missionaries in Africa in the nineteenth century, the 'Ethiopian eunuch', who appears in the Acts of the Apostles (Acts 8:26–39) as the first African convert to Christianity, became an inspiration throughout the continent. Local believers who tired of the paternalism and racism of the mission churches founded African-led 'Ethiopian' churches across Africa.

In addition, the comparatively successful Ethiopian resistance to colonialism that culminated in its victory over the Italians in the Battle of Adwa in 1896 further strengthened the pride of Africans, whether residing in the diaspora or the continent itself. In a period of continent-wide conquest, and worldwide discrimination against people of African descent, Ethiopia appeared as a beacon of freedom and independence. The relatively brief Fascist occupation of the country from 1935 to 1941 did not seriously tarnish its aura.[7]

The rise to power of the charismatic Emperor Haile Selassie I, who cultivated contacts with the African diaspora, added yet another layer to the prestige of the country. This was most notable in Jamaica, where the Ras Tafari (prior to ascending to the throne in 1930 Haile Selassie was Ras (Prince) Täfäri Mäkʷännən) developed an intricate Afrocentric mythology in which he played a major role.[8] It is no accident that Bob Marley and the Wailers' 1976 song 'War' incorporates parts of the emperor's speech delivered to the United Nations on 4 October 1963.

> that until the philosophy which holds one race superior and another inferior is finally and permanently discredited and abandoned; that until there are no longer first-class and second-class citizens of any nation; that until the color of a man's skin is of no more significance than the color of his eyes; that until the basic human rights are equally guaranteed to all without regard to race; that until that day, the dream of lasting peace and world citizenship and the rule of international morality will remain but a fleeting illusion, to be pursued but never attained.[9]

Yet, another vivid expression of Ethiopia's 'African-ness' was that in May 1963 the Organization of African Unity was established in the Ethiopian capital of Addis Ababa with 32 countries as members. It was disbanded in July 2022, but by then it had been replaced by the African Union, a continental organization consisting of 55 countries, which like its predecessor had its permanent secretariat in Addis.

What's in a name?

Any discussion of early Ethiopia must begin by clarifying several issues of terminology, geography and identity. Over the centuries, various terms have been used to designate the area of the Horn of Africa. Among these are India (Hind), Abyssinia (Habash), Kush and, of course, Ethiopia. Repeatedly in this book, I quote sources that refer to the area by one of these names. I have made every

The Horn of Africa.

attempt to minimize the confusion and have in every instance attempted to explain the usage. Immediately below I offer some preliminary clarifications.

Kush and Aithiopía

The term Kush (*Kʾšʾ(i)*), indicating the region south of Egypt (the second cataract on the Nile), first appears almost 3,000 years ago in ancient Egyptian inscriptions. From there the term found its way into numerous ancient languages, including Middle Babylonian, Meroitic, Persian, Syriac, Arabic, Hebrew and Gəʿəz (Ethiopic).

The Hebrew Bible contains numerous mentions of Kush or Kushites and the term 'Kush' refers to several different locations. Already in Genesis 2:13 we read, 'The name of the second river is Gihon; it is the one which flows around the whole land of [K] Cush.'[10] While Ethiopian exegetes and some traditional Jewish sources have argued that this is a reference to the Nile, others believe that, given its wider context, this must refer to the Fertile Crescent and ancient Mesopotamia.[11]

Elsewhere, most notably the Book of Esther 1:1, the term seems to refer to the ends of the Earth: 'In the days of Ahasu-e'rus, the Ahasu-e'rus who reigned from India to Ethiopia [Kush] over one hundred and twenty-seven provinces.' Often, however, Kush refers to a Nubian kingdom, which was situated along the Nile, south of Egypt, and was of particular significance to biblical authors from 747 to 656 BCE.[12] During this period, rulers originally based in what is today Sudan ruled Egypt, as part of the 25th dynasty, and became involved in the global politics of the day.

In Isaiah 37:9 one finds: 'Now the king [Sennacherib, king of Assyria] heard concerning Tirha'kah king of Ethiopia [Kush], "He has set out to fight against you."' When the Hebrew Bible was translated into Greek, the Hebrew *Kush* was translated by the Greek *Aἰθιοπία* (*Aithiopía*) and in this text at least it inherited all the ambiguities of the Hebrew term.

The Greek term *aithiops* – 'blaze' or 'burnt face' – identifies African peoples as darker-skinned than their Greek counterparts. Although several scholars, including writer and scholar J.R.R. Tolkien, have viewed this as an etiological explanation, the origin of the term is not my concern here.[13]

There is a general agreement among scholars that references in classical literature to *Aithiopía* or *Aithiopíans*, whether Homer's 'blameless Ethiopians' or Herodotus' 'the biggest most beautiful and long-lived of men', denote neither modern Ethiopia nor the highland peoples who were the ancestors of the present-day inhabitants of the Ethiopian plateau.[14] Indeed, the term was often used for any area in Africa or specifically for that area south of Egypt and even for places farther afield. As in the Bible, throughout much of history the term was frequently used to refer to Nubia.[15]

India

In classical Greek and Latin, the term 'India' was used to designate a multiplicity of geographic areas. Certainly, it often designated the basin of the Indus river.[16] However, over the course of time and through the division of the distant areas into three separate realms of Greater India, Lesser India and Middle India, the terms were used to reference a series of locations, including not only the Indian subcontinent and the areas of the Indus valley, but such Red Sea countries as South Arabia, Somalia and Ethiopia.

Although at a very early stage (the second century BCE or earlier) ancient authors were aware of the distinction between what we would today refer to as India, and Arabia or Ethiopia, the broader use of the designation 'India' proved remarkably durable. From the earliest accounts of the introduction of Christianity into the Horn of Africa to the arrival of the Portuguese more than a thousand years later, the term persisted. The fascinating discussions of Ethiopian Christians who visited and resided in Rome generally referred to them as Indians.[17] Anyone familiar with the accounts of how Native Americans or 'first peoples' became 'Indians' will not find this confusion surprising. In antiquity, it appears that the conflation of the two areas was related to their geographic extremity, the great rivers (the Nile and the Ganges) which flowed through them, their residents' dark skin, the trade in exotic spices and the presence of 'unusual' animals, particularly elephants, in both places.[18]

Abyssinia (Gəʿəz: Ḥabäśa; Arabic: al- Ḥabäša)

Abyssinia has two distinct meanings: (1) until the middle of the twentieth century it was used as a synonym for the Christian kingdom of 'Ethiopia', and (2) it is also a designation for the predominantly Christian and Semitic-language people of the Ethiopian highlands and Eritrea. Even today, northern Ethiopians and Eritreans who speak one of these countries' Semitic languages refer to themselves as *Habashat*.

The term 'Abyssinia' is derived from Arabic but may date back as far as the second millennium BCE and hieroglyphic Egyptian. Although it has been claimed that the root *al- Ḥabäša* in classical Arabic refers to a collection or 'mixture' of people and was used to describe the multi-ethnic/multilingual nature of the country, this is almost certainly (like the burnt-face *Aithiopia* above) a secondary etymology.[19]

The Ethiopians

Bearing all of this in mind, and even though I weighed alternative titles, including the Habesha or even the Abyssinians, ultimately I felt that only the title 'The Ethiopians' would fit within the rubric of the Lost Civilizations series and attract the appropriate audience. I am, however, painfully aware of the issues raised by this title. I must mention, immediately, that there are other well-known books with the same title, two notable ones written by the distinguished British scholars Edward Ullendorff and Richard Pankhurst.[20]

As Christopher Clapham astutely commented, the seemingly self-evident term 'The Ethiopians' raises complex issues:

> Are they the various 'nationalities' which, since the introduction of the country's present constitution in 1994, have enjoyed formal rights of self-government, and of self-determination, up to and including secession? Do 'Ethiopians' encompass only the Amharic- and Tigrinya-speaking northern highlanders, characterised by adherence to Orthodox Christianity and to a tradition of statehood derived from the Axumite empire of nearly two millennia ago? Or do these peoples change, with the fluctuating boundaries of the Ethiopian state? Are highland Eritreans, ethnically inseparable from Tigrinya-speaking Ethiopians across the frontier, to be included, though they have formed part of an independent state since 1993? Are Ogadeni Somalis, alien to the country's statist traditions but included within its territory, to be left out?[21]

During the period covered by this book until about 1500 most of the southern regions which were conquered by Emperor Mənilək II in the late nineteenth century were not part of the Ethiopian state, and the people in these regions certainly did not identify as Ethiopians. They have, therefore, largely been omitted. However, I have attempted to incorporate the history of Muslim peoples and to a lesser extent the followers of local religions of the region in my discussion.

Moreover, in a recent book, Adam Simmons argued that the people of the region did not refer to themselves as 'Ethiopians' until the fourteenth century![22] So the use of the term may well be anachronistic not only because many of the events that I describe took place in what is today Eritrea, but because even further south the locals did not view themselves as 'Ethiopians'.

Borders

I cannot move any further in my discussion without confronting yet another challenge: the toponymy of the region. The borders of the modern Ethiopian state do not coincide with those of earlier kingdoms of the Aksumites, Zag^{w}e and Solomonic rulers. However, there is no alternative easy designation like 'the Indus'. The Blue Nile runs through much of Ethiopia, but also continues through other countries before reaching the Mediterranean.

Over the course of time the political situation in the Ethiopian highlands varied between periods of strong and expansive centralized rule and weak, fragmented decentralization. The area of influence of the state expanded and contracted. Most of the southern regions of modern Ethiopia have only been firmly (at times violently) integrated into the country's political and economic systems in the past 125 years. Moreover, to the north, the status of Eritrea was the subject of violent dispute throughout most of the twentieth century. At various points throughout this book, I have provided maps to illustrate the areas under discussion during a particular period.

Who were/are the Ethiopians?

Anyone who has read Christina Riggs's excellent book in this series, *Egypt*, will be familiar with the racial controversies that have impacted many discussions of that country and its inhabitants.[23] Although less well known, Ethiopia has been the subject of similar disputes.

In European writing, the idea that the Ethiopians were not Black Africans dates back at least to the late eighteenth century and Edward Gibbon's *The History of the Decline and Fall of the Roman Empire*:

> The friends of the Roman Empire, the Axumites, or Abyssinians, may always be distinguished from the original natives of Africa. The hand of nature has flattened the noses of the negroes, covered their heads with shaggy wool, and tinged their skin with inherent and indelible blackness. But the olive complexion of the Abyssinians, their hair, shape and features, distinctly mark them as a colony of Arabs.[24]

Gibbon's views were echoed, albeit in a less harsh fashion, by the Italian scholar Carlo Conti Rossini, a towering figure in the development of Ethiopian studies in Europe, who viewed early Aksumite civilization as largely the product of culturally superior immigrants from South Arabia.[25] I shall have more to say about this claim in Chapter Two, where I discuss the emergence of early Aksum. I strongly argue for the position that while South Arabians were present in the Horn of Africa and relations between the two sides of the Red Sea were an important political and cultural theme, there is little evidence supporting the idea that Aksumite civilization derived directly from the cultures across the Red Sea. For the moment, let it suffice to say that I warmly accept the conceptualizations of Stuart Munro-Hay in *Aksum: An African Civilisation of Late Antiquity* and David W. Phillipson, *Foundations of an African Civilisation: Aksum and the Northern Horn, 1000 BC–AD 1300*.[26]

In search of ancient Ethiopians

Obviously, the Ethiopians are not in a simple sense a 'lost' people. While one rarely encounters modern Etruscans, Aztecs, Hittites or Barbarians (well, perhaps barbarians!), there are millions of present-day Ethiopians. There is, moreover, considerable cultural and geographic continuity between modern Ethiopia and Eritrea and the same regions dating back over 2,000 years. However, in several senses the earliest periods of Ethiopian history, particularly until around 1500, remain obscure and forgotten.

Despite this rich history as a meeting point of civilizations, Ethiopia and its neighbours have not usually received the attention one might expect. Academically, Ethiopia sometimes falls 'between two stools': neither Middle Eastern enough for those interested in Islam, Arabic language and the politics of oil, nor African enough for those seeking the 'Black Atlantic' of the transatlantic slave trade or the widespread culture of the Swahili coast. Moreover, because it was conquered only briefly, it is not an obvious part of the colonial inheritance of any of the major European powers, and hence not a natural part of their 'overseas' history.

The Kingdom of Aksum was considered one of the four great powers in the third century by the Persian prophet Mani, alongside Persia, Rome and China.[27] Moreover, the Aksumite kingdom played a major role in the superpower struggles of the sixth century in the Red Sea basin. Yet, for much of its subsequent history the Horn of Africa remained relatively unknown to outsiders.

Once again, we can quote from Gibbon's *Decline and Fall*, where he notes that after these sixth-century Aksumite interactions with Arabia, Persia and Byzantium, Ethiopia largely faded from the Western world's historical awareness. 'Encompassed on all sides by enemies of their religion, the Ethiopians slept for near a thousand years, forgetful of the world by whom they were forgotten.'[28] Simmons has recently phrased this more judiciously: 'In the case of Africa . . . almost nothing was recorded by contemporary Latin Christians regarding either Nubia or Ethiopia between the seventh and eleventh century.'[29] Thus these centuries were labelled something of a 'Dark Ages'. This is clearly a misnomer.

Even in discussions of Ethiopian history, the period until 1500 and in some cases even later has often been neglected. Thus despite important scholarship, which I cite below, books on the history of Ethiopia often spend more space discussing the past 150 years of 'modern' history than the previous 1,500 years.[30]

There is, moreover, another sense in which early Ethiopia can be said to have been 'lost'. Although there is a popular narrative of continuity from at least the beginning of the Common Era to the late twentieth century, recent scholarship has constructed a far more complicated picture.[31] While there is a clear case for enduring cultural elements and themes, in numerous respects many details of early Ethiopian history and culture can be shown to have been reconstructed centuries after the events in question, based on much later models and ideologies. Thus we must be careful not to interject later realities into our understanding of the distant past.

The challenge of placing Ethiopian cultural elements in their historical context can perhaps best be illustrated by the consideration of 'traditional' Ethiopian food. As James C. McCann has astutely noted, 'We have to struggle a bit to imagine the tastes and smells of Ethiopia's cooking without its range of spices, colors and pungent combinations of these. These elements, however, were not primordial, but historical.'[32]

For example, although the Portuguese complained that Ethiopian food was spicy, prior to the early sixteenth century this was not because of the ubiquitous *Capsicum frutescens* peppers (*berbere*) which give so much northern food its typical 'heat' and red colour (*qay*). These peppers, which are native to South or Central America, only arrived in Europe, Africa and the Middle East in the early sixteenth century, after the beginning of the 'Columbian exchange' with the New World. Somewhat more speculatively, it has recently been argued that while the staple crop of *ṭeff* (*Eragrostis tef*) certainly grew in the Horn for millennia, consumption of this grain greatly increased over a period of 250 years from the 1520s and that the round, pancake-like *ṭeff* flatbreads known as *ənǧära* became the staple food of northern Ethiopia only in the early 1750s.[33]

We are on much firmer ground when we turn to coffee. According to a widespread tradition a shepherd in the south-western Käfa region of Ethiopia first discovered the effects of the plant through the erratic behaviour of his goats, who consumed the bean. (Other strains appear to have developed in other parts of Africa.) This specific story, though, is not firmly documented before the seventeenth century. The kernel of truth here would appear to be the origin of the plant in this area. However, the earliest records we have of these beans being brewed date from the fifteenth century. Moreover, because of its association with Islam and spirit cults, Ethiopian Christians did not consume it. Only in the late nineteenth century did this change and the famous Ethiopian 'coffee ceremony' develop.[34]

Field of *ṭeff*.

While it is certainly not my intention to deprive anyone of the pleasure of consuming 'traditional', 'authentic' Ethiopian food at their local restaurant, or of imbibing delicious coffee, I cite these ideas to stress how easy it is to accept the antiquity, even the primordiality, of elements that developed under specific historical circumstances. One of the challenges of this book is to disrupt many such assumptions not primarily in the realm of food but rather in the presentation and reception of historical events and the emergence of cultural elements.

I argue that the sacred geography of ancient Aksum, the fourth-century ruler 'Ezana's conversion to Christianity, the stories of Syrian monks who came to Ethiopia in the fifth and sixth centuries, the location of the grave of the Aksumite king who welcomed the first Muslims, the musical innovations of St Yared, and the achievements of the Zagʷe dynasty have all been shaped (nay, even distorted!) by a much later 'medieval' perspective.[35] When European observers came to the area in the fifteenth century and later, they often assumed that what they saw had remained unchanged for centuries. In some cases, however, the rituals, structures and texts they described were no more than a few decades old.

The ancient past has thus been 'lost', or perhaps a better phrase would be 'hidden' or refracted through a later lens. A major part of this book will be the attempt to revisit and reframe these early events. As much as possible, I have sought to present what has been until quite recently the scholarly consensus on a particular period, event or process and then explain the reasons why I believe that this earlier narrative should be revisited.

In my opening chapter, I consider the diverse and sometimes contradictory images of the mysterious Queen of Sheba, or as she is known in Ethiopia and Eritrea, Makədda. The second chapter examines the factors behind the rise of the Aksumite kingdom and in particular attempts to debunk the notion that Aksum was merely an offshoot of early South Arabian culture and civilization. I also turn my attention to the port of Adulis and the broader context of ancient Ethiopia and Eritrea in the world of the Red Sea–Indian Ocean trade networks. In Chapter Three, I consider the sources that have survived for the entry of Christianity to the Aksumite kingdom and attempt to piece them together in a manner that does justice to this important change but does not overemphasize its immediate impact on society and state.

The fourth chapter is perhaps the most complicated and challenging. In the early fifth century CE the Aksumite rulers represented a powerful trading polity on the Red Sea. Their position was not unrivalled and clashes and skirmishes with their opponents along and across the sea were frequent. These reached their peak circa 522, when a Jewish or at least 'Judaized' ruler of Ḥimyar massacred Christians in a town called Nağrān. The Ethiopian emperor Kaleb, prompted by the Byzantine emperor Justin I (518–27), set out to protect his faith on behalf of the Christian world and was victorious. Despite his initial success, Aksumite power soon waned. Moreover, in the changing political environment the new forces of Islam and the Persians made maintenance of Aksumite supremacy impossible. Eventually the Aksumite kingdom declined and the period from the eighth to the eleventh century is still not well understood. Nevertheless, this political decline did not result in a cultural crisis and many elements of Aksumite political and religious life persisted.

Under a dynasty usually referred to as the Zagʷe, but perhaps more appropriately designated as the rulers of Bəgʷəna (Bugna), powerful Christian leaders made their influence felt in many parts of the highlands. Although later history written by their opponents dismissed the Zagʷe as usurpers, recent historical research has dramatically revised this position. I present a summary of this new understanding in Chapter Five.

The eleventh and twelfth centuries can now be seen as marking a revival of Christianity and a strengthening of its institutions. Ties with the Egyptian Coptic Church appear to have been particularly close. Vast energy was invested in building churches and other structures, not only in the major town, which came to be named after the famous ruler Lalibäla, but in Təgray and Eritrea. At the same time, Muslim settlement in the Horn became an important cultural theme for the region.

Until recently, the rise of the Zagʷe has been seen as a rupture in Ethiopian history, a break from the Semitic-based traditions of Aksum. However, in the past decade new research has dramatically challenged this view and in many ways upended the usual narrative of early and medieval Ethiopian history. There can be little question that Marie-Laure Derat's *L'énigme d'une dynastie sainte et usurpatrice dans le royaume chrétien d'Éthiopie du XIe au XIIIe siècle* is the most important book on early Ethiopian history written in more than half a century.[36] A valuable composition, it not only transforms our understanding of the Zagʷe but provides a dramatic pivot point for the entire narrative that begins with Aksum. The Zagʷe now appear, far more than has been previously recognized, to have been heirs of Aksumite traditions.

It now seems (or so I shall argue) that the rise to power of a new upstart dynasty based in Amhara in 1270, which depicted itself as the heir to Aksum and of a Solomonic tradition, represents a far more dramatic shift in power than that of the Zagʷe. These new rulers claimed to be the heirs to both the Aksumite rulers and Solomon and Sheba. It was a brilliant piece of 'identity theft' in which their rise to power was depicted as a 'restoration' of the most ancient and venerable symbols of northern Ethiopia. From 1270 on powerful rulers expanded the lands under their dominion, subdued their opponents regardless of what religion they professed, and gained military and economic control of a vastly expanded kingdom.

In this context, it must be noted that this southern move can only be understood in the context of important changes in the history of Islam in the region. The Dahlak islands off the coast of modern-day Eritrea were initially the primary conduit for the passage of Muslims into the interior. In the twelfth century the entry point shifted to the southern port of Zaylaʿ. This not only led to the development of new trade routes but was probably crucial in the shift of Christian power southwards.

A little more than a century after this dynastic change we enter what many have seen as a 'Golden Age' in Ethiopian history.[37] As I discuss in Chapter Seven, although the rise to power of Emperor Dawit II in 1380 does not mark a dramatic shift in power, under his rule and those of his sons spectacular changes took place within Ethiopian Christianity. Calendric reforms, cultic innovations, literary initiatives and new artistic achievements all led to transformations in Christian life. It would not be an exaggeration to speak of a 'Dawitian' or 'Yaʿqobian' Church, based on the achievements of his son, Zär'a Yaʿqob (r. 1434–68).[38]

Although the end of the fifteenth century does not mark the end of our story, it is convenient to conclude this book a little beyond 1500. The Ottomans' conquest of Egypt and their involvement in the Red Sea basin was rivalled by the Europeans who began to arrive in the region. The Islamic principalities of the Horn saw dramatic changes in their political orientation, with militant clerics gaining the upper hand and challenging the political dominance of the Christian kingdom. The Oromo people, today the largest single ethnic group in Ethiopia, began to expand northwards and challenge the cultural and military hegemony of the Christian kingdom.

The nature and quantity of our source materials change. Not surprisingly, in the 'Age of Discovery' the Ethiopians can hardly be claimed to be a 'lost' civilization. When I began to write this book, I naively thought that it would be an easy task, demanding that I do little more than summarize the existing scholarship; update the findings of Ullendorff, Pankhurst and other important scholars based on new findings; and choose appropriate illustrations. I anticipated that my greatest challenge would be finding a way to incorporate the existing information within the limits of a comparatively short volume for an educated, but non-specialist, reader. In this respect it would resemble in some ways *Les Falâshâs*, which I wrote over thirty years ago as part of a series on Fils d'Abraham.[39]

I could not have been more wrong. In this respect this book is much closer to my study of Betä Ǝsr'ael history, which challenged much of the accepted narrative.[40] The recent scholarship, as well as shifting perspectives on the region, have made this book challenging, demanding and rewarding. As anyone perusing each chapter's references and bibliography will note, new research of major relevance to my concerns continues to appear at a rapid pace. Often, I felt as if I was trying to navigate not by gazing at the stars but by looking at fast-moving clouds.

It is difficult to exaggerate the importance of the research that has appeared in the quarter-century since Pankhurst's book was published. Beginning with the Ethiopian Manuscript Microfilm Project, which was initiated in the 1970s, a series of research projects have been undertaken to visit Ethiopia and Eritrea's monastic libraries and to photograph manuscripts.[41] As technology progressed, not only did it become far easier to make copies of manuscripts, but these were digitized and made available online. Existing collections of manuscripts in European libraries became accessible along with hundreds of manuscripts in relatively isolated Ethiopian and Eritrean church libraries.

There was no longer a need to purchase or abscond with manuscript treasures as arrangements could be negotiated to photograph the works in question. Thus numerous previously unknown works were photographed and identified. At the same time, compositions that had previously been known through, at most, a handful of manuscripts, or even leaves scattered in different libraries, could now be examined through dozens and even hundreds of exemplars. Inevitably, claims and conclusions that had previously been based with a fair degree of confidence, and even hubris, on a limited sample size have had to be revised.

During most of the period from 1974 to 1991 conditions in the Horn made it extremely difficult to conduct fieldwork, whether anthropological or archaeological. Once again, the past three decades have seen a dramatic improvement in research conditions. Although security considerations remain a concern, much pioneering work has been accomplished. In particular, excavations have extended beyond the traditional fields of prehistory and antiquity to later historical periods.[42] Technological advances have made it possible to glean new information, and progress has been made in the archaeology of Islam in the region, which has greatly improved our understanding of this religion and its social, historical and cultural environment.[43]

Let us end here on a few technical notes. The transliteration of Gəʿəz, Amharic, Təgrayanʿ and other foreign-language terms are based on the norms established by the *Encyclopaedia Aethiopica*. However, there are a few exceptions. In cases in which there is a familiar accepted version of a personal or geographic name, such as Haile Selassie (rather than Ḥaylä Śəllase), Eritrea and obviously Ethiopia, these forms have been adopted. Moreover, in several cases such as Däbrä Dammo and Zär'a Yaʿqob I have used slightly different forms than the *Encyclopaedia* in keeping with the most recent scholarly usage.

Dates are given according to the Gregorian Calendar, which is eight years different from the Ethiopian Julian calendar. (Thus the beginning of the third millennium according to the Ethiopian Calendar was marked on New Year's 2000, which coincided with 11 September 2007 in the Gregorian calendar.) The forms BCE and CE are used rather than BC and AD.

ONE

The Many Faces of the Queen of Sheba

In May 2008 a wide variety of news sources breathlessly reported that a team of archaeologists from the University of Hamburg had located the palace of the biblical Queen of Sheba, as well as an altar which may have once held the treasured Ark of the Covenant.[1] (Almost immediately, another team of researchers based at the same university's Hiob Ludolf Centre for Ethiopian and Eritrean Studies issued a press release, dismissing the claim and in particular disassociating themselves from their colleagues' assertions.[2]) Eventually, the first group clarified that what they had uncovered was probably a large mansion, but speculated that the Queen's palace might lie beneath their excavation site.

Not to be outdone, four years later a team of British archaeologists claimed they had found – again in northern Ethiopia – the gold mine from which the Queen brought gold to Jerusalem.[3] (See Psalm 72:10: 'The kings of Sheba and Seba shall offer gifts.') And in the same year the BBC, apparently referencing an article published four years earlier in the *American Journal of Human Genetics*, claimed that DNA confirmed (or at least supported) the Sheba story. Professor Chris Tyler-Smith of the Wellcome Sanger Institute in Cambridge told BBC News: 'By analysing the genetics of Ethiopia and several other regions we can see that there was gene flow into Ethiopia, probably from the Levant, around 3,000 years ago, and this fits perfectly with the story of the Queen of Sheba.'[4] Oh, that it was so simple!

Even today, scholars have not reached a consensus regarding the historicity of the Queen or her place of origin. Dubbed by *National Geographic* 'the Greta Garbo of antiquity',[5] many believe her to have come from the ancient South Arabian kingdom of Saba, which was in what is, today, Yemen. However, she has also been claimed to be from southern Africa, in the region of modern Zimbabwe, and even as far afield as southwest Nigeria among the Yoruba people. After excavations in Nigeria in 1999, the archaeologist Patrick Darling was quoted as saying, 'I don't want to overplay the Sheba theory, but it cannot be discounted . . . The local people believe it and that's what is important.'[6]

Biblical roots

The story of the Queen of Sheba first appears in two slightly different biblical versions: 1 Kings 10:1–13 and 2 Chronicles 9:1–12. In both places the text offers only the sparsest of narratives: the Queen of Sheba, having heard of Solomon's greatness, travelled to Jerusalem to test him with difficult questions. She brought with her gold, spices and precious stones. Solomon won her over not only by answering her questions but through the evidence of his well-managed court, his palace and the Temple. The Queen blessed God and gave Solomon gifts from the riches she had brought. (There is a short mention of gold from Ophir brought by the navy of King Hiram, as well as almug trees used in the construction of the Temple and his palace.) After Solomon reciprocated the Queen returned to her land.

> 1 Kings 10:1–13
> **1** And when the queen of Sheba heard of the fame of Solomon concerning the name of the LORD, she came to prove him with hard questions.
> **2** And she came to Jerusalem with a very great train, with camels that bare [*sic*] spices, and very much gold, and precious stones: and when she was come to Solomon, she communed with him of all that was in her heart.
> **3** And Solomon told her all her questions: there was not any thing hid from the king, which he told her not.
> **4** And when the queen of Sheba had seen all Solomon's wisdom, and the house that he had built,

5 And the meat of his table, and the sitting of his servants, and
the attendance of his ministers, and their apparel, and his cup-
bearers, and his ascent by which he went up unto the house of
the LORD; there was no more spirit in her.
6 And she said to the king, It was a true report that I heard in
mine own land of thy acts and of thy wisdom.
7 Howbeit I believed not the words, until I came, and mine
eyes had seen it: and, behold, the half was not told me: thy
wisdom and prosperity exceedeth the fame which I heard.
8 Happy are thy men, happy are these thy servants, which
stand continually before thee, and that hear thy wisdom.
9 Blessed be the LORD thy God, which delighted in thee, to set
thee on the throne of Israel: because the LORD loved Israel for
ever, therefore made he thee king, to do judgment and justice.
10 And she gave the king one hundred and twenty talents of
gold, and of spices very great store, and precious stones: there
came no more such abundance of spices as these which the
queen of Sheba gave to king Solomon.
11 And the navy also of Hiram, that brought gold from Ophir,
brought in from Ophir great plenty of almug trees, and precious stones.
12 And the king made of the almug trees pillars for the house
of the LORD, and for the king's house, harps also and psalteries
for singers: there came no such almug trees, nor were seen
unto this day.
13 And king Solomon gave unto the queen of Sheba all her
desire, whatsoever she asked, beside that which Solomon gave
her of his royal bounty. So she turned and went to her own
country, she and her servants.

As is often the case, the very brevity of the biblical narrative seems to have encouraged the development of legendary elaborations on the story. Muslim, Jewish, medieval Christian and, of course, Ethiopian sources have added vivid details to the concise and circumspect biblical story.

Although the Hebrew Bible speaks of the Queen of Sheba (Malkaṯ Šəḇā), this is only one of the names by which she is known. The New Testament (Matthew 12:42; Luke 11:31) tells, 'The Queen of the South shall rise up in judgment with this generation, and shall condemn it: for she came from the uttermost parts of the earth to hear the wisdom of Solomon.'

The *Testament of Solomon*, a Greek pseudepigraphic text from sometime between the third and fifth centuries CE, has Solomon offering a very different take on the Queen's character:

> And among them also the Queen of the South, being a witch, came in great concern and bowed low before me to the earth. And having heard my wisdom, she glorified the God of Israel, and she made formal trial of all my wisdom, of all love in which I instructed her, according to the wisdom imparted to me. And all the sons of Israel glorified God.[7]

In Islamic traditions the Queen is known as Bilqis and the tests she poses to Solomon are depicted as an attempt to blur the essential categories of the divinely organized universe. Thus she challenges him to distinguish similarly clothed young men and women from each other; to distinguish between real flowers and imitations. For her part she is unable to differentiate between real water and a skilfully manufactured mirror. Her semi-demonic nature is revealed by her hairy, goat-like legs. All of this appears to be an attempt to highlight that she is an anomaly and herself violates the divine order by virtue of her being a female ruler.[8]

Some Christian sources credit the Queen with bringing the wood of the Cross to Jerusalem or compare the gifts she brought to Solomon with those later presented to the Christ child by her descendants, the Three Wise Men (Magi).[9] (Who, as we shall see below, were also believed to be ancestors of another legendary Ethiopian ruler, Prester John.)

She has inspired such different authors as the novelist Rudyard Kipling, the adventure writer H. Rider Haggard and the African nationalist and first president of Senegal Léopold Senghor. With changing standards of female attractiveness and racial identity, she has been depicted in films by a series of beautiful women, including the Italian actress Gina Lollobrigida (1959) and later Academy

Gina Lollobrigida as Queen of Sheba in *Solomon and Sheba* (1959, dir. King Vidor).

Halle Berry as Queen of Sheba in *Solomon and Sheba* (1995, dir. Robert M. Young).

Award winner Halle Berry (1995) and Vivica A. Fox (1997), both of whom are African American.[10] In the 2022 film *Three Thousand Years of Longing*, she was portrayed by the Ugandan actress and model Aamito Lagum.

Thus in a period of slightly more than sixty years she has gone from being imagined as a southern European to a sub-Saharan African. Her racial identity is, of course, part of a larger debate regarding both her country of origin and, if she is Ethiopian, the African-ness of Ethiopians.

In the middle of the eighteenth century Georg Friedrich Händel included the lively 'Arrival of the Queen of Sheba' in the opening of the third act of his oratorio *Solomon*. It is still played at many weddings (think Lady Edith's wedding in the final episode of *Downton Abbey*). More than two centuries later, the government of the Yemen Arab Republic (now the Republic of Yemen) celebrated the premiere performance of the operetta *The Queen of Sheba Dam*, which offered an overview of 2,500 years of Yemenite history. Working on the other side of the Red Sea, entrepreneurs and investors have recently christened Ethiopia's ambitious tech centre Sheba Valley!

Kəbrä Nägäśt

The Ethiopian version of the Sheba story – *Kəbrä Nägäśt* (The Glory of Kings) – is unique in several respects. The Queen is known in Ethiopian tradition as Makədda, which may be derived from either 'Macedonian', as in Alexander the Great of Macedon, or Candace, from the title of the queens of Meroë, a city in Kush, the remains of which are found in modern-day Sudan. The latter seeks to identify her with the Queen of the Ethiopians mentioned in Acts 8:27, whose servant was an early convert to Christianity.

Not only is this the lengthiest and most elaborate of the Sheba legends, but it differs significantly from the others in purpose and function. If elsewhere the primary focus of the story is Solomon's wisdom and miraculous powers, the Ethiopian text is concerned with the Queen, her son Mənilək, and the transfer of the mantle of God's chosen people to the Ethiopians. If elsewhere the Sheba legend represents a minor topic within a vast corpus of legendary material, in Ethiopia it stands at the heart of the country's religio-political traditions.

According to the *Kəbrä Nägäśt*, having heard of Solomon's great wisdom, Makədda travelled from Aksum to visit Solomon in Jerusalem. During her stay, Solomon not only dazzled her with his wisdom, but tricked her by a ruse into having sexual relations with him. The Queen conceived a son, whom she bore upon her return to Aksum. When he reached maturity, this son, Mənilək, journeyed to Jerusalem to meet his father. At the completion of his visit, Solomon commanded that the first-born sons of the priests and elders of Israel accompany Mənilək back to Aksum. Before setting out, however, his companions, led by 'Azaryah, the son of the High Priest, stole the Ark of the Covenant from the Temple. Thus the glory of Zion passed from Jerusalem and the Children of Israel to the new Zion, Aksum, and the new Israel, the Ethiopian people.

The story is engaging, at points even amusing. Yet its occasional lightness of tone should not lead us to underestimate its centrality for an understanding of the thought-world of traditional Ethiopia. For the country's ruling elites, the *Kəbrä Nägäśt* inscribed the basic categories of the political–religious order.

Not only was royal legitimacy linked to a direct descent from Solomon and Sheba, but Ethiopia's nobility and priests were seen as part of a divinely ordained world order. While many Christian groups have claimed to be *Verus Israel* (True Israel), for Ethiopian Christians this was not merely a spiritual claim but a biological fact.

There is still a lively scholarly debate regarding the dating of the *Kəbrä Nägäśt*. Some place it as early as the sixth century CE, while others believe it surfaced or resurfaced in Gəʿəz in the early fourteenth century. It must be pointed out that even those who suggest an early date for the text place it more than 1,500 years after the reign of King Solomon!

At least in part, the controversy regarding the date of the *Kəbrä Nägäśt* appears to revolve around a certain lack of precision regarding terminology and the framing of the question. It is comparatively easy to identify elements within the *Kəbrä Nägäśt* that might be dated as early as the sixth century CE. Emperor Kaleb, who on several occasions invaded South Arabia and established Aksumite sovereignty there, explicitly associated himself with the Davidic line in an inscription on a stele erected in the important South Arabian city of Marib. Writing in Greek and Gəʿəz, he claims he was called to war like David against the Amalekites [*sic*], and that he possessed the 'glory of David' (*Kəbrä Dawit*). This is, of course, a far cry from a claim to Solomonic descent, much less the pilfering of the Ark of the Covenant from the Temple.

In the twelfth century Abu l-Makarum Sa'ada, a Coptic priest, was familiar with the idea that Abyssinia was the home of the Queen of Sheba, and that the Abyssinians possessed the Ark of the Covenant, but Stuart Munro-Hay suggested that the Ethiopians' claim to have this valuable relic was very late, because the sixteenth-century Portuguese missionary and explorer Francisco Álvares made no mention of it in his recounting of the Solomon and Sheba saga.[11]

Any visitor to Ethiopia since the earlier twentieth century will have doubtless seen the episodic cartoon-like version of the story

of Solomon and Sheba. Although the precise date of the origins of this art form is unclear, there is only evidence for its existence with the development of early 'tourism' from the first half of the twentieth century. In addition to the kernel of the Solomon–Sheba legend, these images eventually evolved to include other themes. One of these is a Təgrayan tale that recounts how in ancient times the Ethiopians worshipped a great serpent, which was eventually killed. (This story is also recounted in the origin story of Ethiopia's oldest monastery, Däbrä Dammo.) At the other end of

Painting on cotton depicting scenes from the story of Solomon and Sheba by an unknown Ethiopian artist, collected 1940s.

the narrative Mənilək's visit to and return from Israel as well as the eventual death of his mother are depicted.

Over the decades a standard pattern emerged with 44 panels being the most usual, but far from the only, presentation. In many cases anachronistic touches were introduced such as firearms and European elements. (In a large depiction of the Queen's arrival in Jerusalem on the wall of the Ethiopian Orthodox Church's chapel above the Church of the Holy Sepulchre in the Old City of Jerusalem, some of Solomon's Jewish countrymen are depicted with the *payot* (side curls) of modern ultra-Orthodox Jews.)

Hebraic–Israelite modelling

The *Kəbrä Nägäśt* serves as a gateway to one of the most discussed aspects of Ethiopian Christianity: its Hebraic–biblical character. Throughout much of their history Ethiopian Christians venerated Saturday, referred to as the 'first Sabbath', as a day of rest alongside the Christian Sunday Sabbath. Male children were circumcised on the eighth day after their birth. Ethiopian Christians did not consume pork.

From the early sixteenth century onwards, Ethiopian churches were traditionally built with a tripartite division which consciously echoed the architecture of the Temple in Jerusalem. The most sacred area of a church is called the *qedussä qeddusan* (Holy of Holies) and within it is the *tabot*, which recalls the original Ark of the Covenant of the Israelites. The *tabot* is dedicated to a saint, angel or one of the many attributes of Mary or Jesus.

Indeed, when the Portuguese arrived in Ethiopia in the sixteenth century they were appalled by the 'Jewish' character of the Ethiopian Church. They viewed Ethiopian Christianity in the context of Iberian battles against *conversos* Jews who while outwardly converted to Christianity continued to secretly practise elements of Judaism, such as abstinence from pork, the practice of circumcision and the veneration of the Sabbath. All these behaviours were seen by Catholics in the sixteenth century as a stubborn refusal by Ethiopian Christians to abandon Jewish behaviours in favour of a 'pure' Christian life.[12]

Scholars have long debated the significance of these elements and when they became an integral part of Ethiopian Christian culture. Some, like Edward Ullendorff, have contended that these are ancient elements which in some cases pre-date the arrival of Christianity in the country. Certainly, some Ethiopian traditions claim that before the acceptance of Christianity, half the population of the country was Jewish. In contrast, the French scholar of Ethiopia, Islam and the Middle East Maxime Rodinson believed that most of these elements date from no more than five or six hundred years ago and are primarily the result of the imitation of the Old Testament rather than of direct contacts with ancient Jews.[13]

Rodinson is probably correct in most respects. Ethiopian churches do not appear to have been consistently built according to the plan of the Temple prior to the early sixteenth century. Pork was not eaten by Christians, Muslims or Jews in Ethiopia, so the abstinence from this meat hardly carried with it the powerful social and symbolic significance it held for European Jews and Christians. Many of the 'Jewish–biblical' themes found in Ethiopian Christian literature can be shown to have reached the country after the twelfth century through the mediation of Arabic Christian sources, and not through early direct contact with either local or foreign Jews. Yet, this comparatively late institutionalization does not make these motifs any less striking to any observer more familiar with other forms of Christianity. Ethiopian rulers from the fourteenth century on claimed to be Israelites, descendants of the Queen of Sheba and Solomon, and bore names such as 'Amdä Ṣəyon (the Pillar of Zion), Dawit (David), Yəṣḥaq (Isaac) and Zär'a Ya'qob (Seed of

The Chapel of the Tablet, Aksum.

The Bath of the Queen of Sheba, Aksum.

Jacob). Numerous prayers and homilies celebrate the glory of Zion, which is identified with not only biblical Jerusalem but the earliest Ethiopian capital city, Aksum, the later church city of Lalibäla and the Virgin Mary, whose womb is associated with the Ark of the Covenant. Alongside the country's large Christian population there was for centuries a small Jewish minority, who called themselves Bətä Ǝsra'el (the House of Israel) and claimed to be the remnants of Jewish migrants who had refused to convert to Christianity. Known to outsiders as 'Fälaśa' (Falasha), they claimed this name derived from the fact that they were exiles (*fälasyan*) who had come to Ethiopia as migrants thousands of years ago. Indeed most of these 'Ethiopan Jews', who today have migrated to Israel, still retain one or another version of this origin story.

I began this chapter by citing the conflicting claims of two groups of Hamburg-based scholars regarding the discovery of the Queen of Sheba's palace. It is useful to conclude by returning to the geography of the area around Aksum. Any visitor to Aksum will be shown sites that are associated with the Queen and her son Mənilək. Among the most important is a large pool called the Queen of Sheba's Bath, the shrine said to hold the original Ark of the Covenant, and the Queen's palace.

All these placements are undoubtedly fascinating but certainly date to much later periods than the putative Queen. In saying this I mean no disrespect to the Ethiopian Orthodox Church or its traditions. However, as the French historian Maurice Halbwachs has discussed so brilliantly, the collective memory of the sacred land changes from one generation to another according to the social and historical transformations of each historical present. While Halbwachs was interested primarily in the medieval origin of Christian sites in the 'Holy Land', his insights hold true not only for Aksum and its queen, but, as we shall see, for many other sites throughout Ethiopian history.[14]

TWO
The Rise of Aksum

While the legend of the Queen of Sheba assumes that a centralized monarchy existed in northern Ethiopia and Eritrea from at least a thousand years before the Common Era, historians and archaeologists date the rise of the kingdom of Aksum to the turn of the Common Era.[1] This is not, of course, to claim that the regions of ancient Eritrea and Ethiopia were uninhabited prior to the rise of the Aksumite state.

We are fortunate that for more than 150 years travellers, explorers and scholars have attempted to uncover the roots of civilization in northern Ethiopia and Eritrea. Already in the first half of the twentieth century professional archaeologists encouraged by the reigning Ethiopian emperor Mənilək II (r. 1889–1913) began to conduct systematic excavations in different regions. This activity accelerated from the 1950s on. Indeed, different political regimes supported work on different topics in keeping with their broader cultural policy and vision of the nation.

Much of this work focused on elements associated with the rise of Aksumite culture, the development of Christian civilization and the magnificent rock-hewn churches found at various sites. (The groundbreaking work of prehistory has primarily taken place in southern regions such as ʿAfar and the Omo valley, which were not part of pre-modern Ethiopia. For other reasons, Islamic and early modern archaeology were also neglected until recently.)

Based on these discoveries, scholars have proposed different timelines for the emergence of early civilization in Ethiopia and Eritrea. It is impossible here to discuss and compare all the

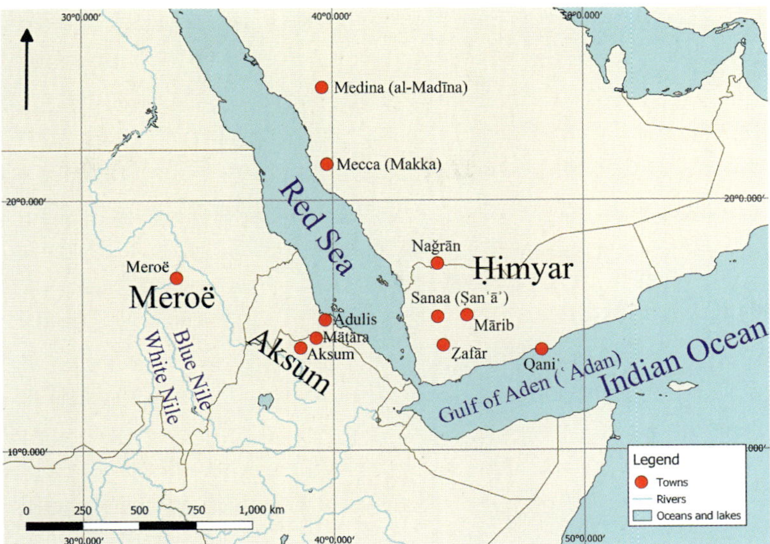

Aksum, Meroë and Himyar.

different periodizations that have been suggested. As I shall discuss below, changing understandings of early history have inevitably produced different chronologies. Some scholars have sought to differentiate between rapidly developing elite culture(s) and relatively stable, broadly based elements. Dissimilarities are also related to the results of excavations carried out at different locations.[2] What follows below is, therefore, inevitably general, and summative.[3]

The land of Punt is mentioned as a trading partner in Egyptian sources as far back as 2500 BCE. Scholars are unclear regarding both the etymology of the designation and the precise location to which it refers. Most believe that the term (Egyptian *Pwn.t*) refers to an area of Africa which overlaps with parts of contemporary Ethiopia, Eritrea, Somalia and perhaps Sudan. Depictions of giraffes, rhinoceroses, leopards and baboons, as well as trade in gold, ebony and ivory, are cited in support of this view. The northern part of the Horn would appear most likely. The decline of a centralized government in Egypt circa 1100 BCE led to the waning of trade with Punt and its survival more in the realm of longing and myth than in practical concerns.

Beginning in the 1960s archaeologists began to uncover the remains of what they called 'Ona Culture', with 'Ona' coming from the Təgrəñña (an Ethio-Semitic language commonly spoken in Eritrea and in northern Ethiopia's Təgray region) word meaning '(ancient) ruins'. More recent excavations near both Asmara and the Təgrayan–Eritrean border have provided fascinating evidence of this early agropastoral culture, which existed in Eritrea and northern Ethiopia from the early to mid-first millennium BCE. Depending on the site, the local population grew *ṭeff*, wheat, barley or lentils and raised cattle, sheep or goats. There is also evidence of ritual life and the small-scale exchange of goods, including gold.

In the Horn of Africa, as elsewhere, the emergence of a centralized political organization was the result of a variety of different local causes. As I indicated in the Prologue to this volume, for many years scholars claimed that the Aksumite state emerged because of external initiatives through which South Arabian institutions and concepts were transplanted to what is today northern Ethiopia and Eritrea. Only two decades ago, in the first volume of the authoritative *Encyclopaedia Aethiopica*, one author wrote of 'sites [that] belong to this "South Arabia" phase in Eritrea and Ethiopia . . . including Aksum itself', while another claimed that 'Ethiopia originated as a colony of the South Arabian kingdom of Saba''.[4] From this perspective the rise of the Aksumite polity and eventually Ethiopian civilization was attributed to the influence, even the initiative, of foreign colonists. Research carried out during the first decades of the twenty-first century has done much to decolonize the depiction of ancient Ethiopia and Eritrea.

Over time the claims of a decisive South Arabian impact have moderated, but the extent of South Arabian influence is still debated. Emblematic of this issue is the character of the primary language for the writing of inscriptions and later literature in Ethiopia. Gəʽəz is a Semitic language related linguistically and historically to South Arabian. It is written in a script (Ethiopic) derived from South Arabian script (Musnad). However, from an early date in the earliest surviving inscriptions it is already possible to distinguish between inscriptions written in a South Arabian language (and script) and contemporary texts written in the same script but conveying a different language which was a precursor of Gəʿəz. Once again, the impact of South Arabian culture is less than had previously been hypothesized.

Much of the discussion about the rise of early Aksumite civilization has centred around the town of Yəḥa in northern Təgray, about 46 kilometres (28½ mi.) northeast of Aksum. Here we find the structure that is most emblematic of the early South Arabian presence in the Horn, the Great Temple dedicated to the Sabaean God of the Moon, Almaqah. Since its 'discovery' by Henry Salt in the early nineteenth century, this monumental structure (18.5 metres long, 15 metres wide and at its peak 13 metres tall (61 × 49¼ × 42½ ft)) has captured the imagination of generations of scholars seeking to uncover the genesis of Aksumite culture.

It is dated to the seventh or eighth century BCE based on similar structures in South Arabia,[5] as well as epigraphic evidence written in a South Arabian script, and associated with the emergence of a polity (or perhaps a people) named Dʿmt.[6] The evidence for South Arabian influences is found in architectural, iconographic and religious characteristics shared with this region, in particular with the kingdom of Sabaʾ.

While it is hard to discount this evidence of a significant South Arabian presence in this area, we must avoid interpretating it as the source of later Aksumite civilization.[7] The influence of Dʿmt on the wider region was extremely limited both chronologically and geographically. While some sites in Eritrea, such as Mäṭära (or Bäläw Qäläw) show South Arabian cultural influence prior to the rise of Aksum, others in the area around present-day Asmara do not.[8] Even in Yəḥa itself South Arabian religious traditions – incense burners, inscriptions and some elements of political culture – existed alongside a much wider indigenous Pre-Aksumite culture. Dʿmt itself seems to have owed a great deal to autochthonal developments and local elites. Briefly stated, the suggestion that Aksum emerged because of a major South Arabian colonization of the Horn of Africa is no longer widely accepted. Indeed, in some cases similar items found on both sides of the Red Sea have now been shown to have developed independently of each other.[9]

Ruins of the Great Temple of Almaqah, Yəḥa.

The development of extensive irrigation systems is yet another important element in the emergence of Aksumite civilization which in the past was viewed as a South Arabian influence. However, recent work centred on an area of 100 square kilometres (39 sq. mi.) around Yəḥa has indicated that there appears to be no direct correlation between irrigation and population centres.[10] This is not to say that water resources were unimportant in the development of northeastern Təgray. As one would expect, early agriculturally based settlements were located with an eye to easy access to water. In some areas, seasonal rainfall appears to have been sufficient, but already in Pre-Aksumite times 'rain harvesting', the collection of rainwater into artificial ponds or on rooftops, was practised.

We are fortunate to have a fair amount of knowledge about the earliest crops raised in these settlements. It should be noted that none of the early sources on Aksum mention the import of food, so the area appears to have been largely self-sufficient.[11] Best-known and historically most valuable is *ṭeff* (or teff), which is highly prized for the making of *ənǧära*, a sour pancake-like bread which has been a staple of northern Ethiopian and Eritrean diets for hundreds of years.[12] *Ṭeff*, which has the tiniest seeds of any grain (about 1 millimetre), is not only rich in protein, but an excellent source of iron, calcium and zinc.[13]

Sabaic inscription from Yəḥa.

It is agreed that sorghum was first domesticated in the savannah zone of present-day Chad and Sudan and its cultivation in Ethiopia and Eritrea dates to before the Common Era. It is interesting to note that in the recent past among the Amhara of central Ethiopia sorghum is viewed as a sign of poverty and has a much lower status than *ṭeff*. Further south it does not carry this opprobrium. Although in the north barley does not have the distinctiveness or symbolic importance of *ṭeff*, among some southern peoples it is said that *gebs yä 'əhəl nəguś*, 'barley is the king of grains.' It was first domesticated in Ethiopia circa 3000 BCE. Ears of wheat are depicted on Aksumite coins, and finger millet also originated in East Africa in the region between Ethiopia and Uganda. Remains of the latter have been uncovered in the Horn along with early pottery from as early as the fourth or third millennium BCE. To these grains must be added various legumes, including lentils and chickpeas. Thus the rise of agricultural economies in the Horn appears to have been based on a variety of crops.

Among the still-unanswered questions about the ancient city of Aksum are the reasons for its specific location. While it has been suggested that the immediate availability of gold may have been a significant factor in promoting urban growth, other less exotic factors may have been more important. Abundant rainfall, soils amenable to a variety of crops, and ample grazing land all appear to have been important. Over time its position as the hub of a radiating network of river valleys, facilitating a complex system of communication and exchange, was also of major importance.[14]

A sea on the way to somewhere else

Moving away from the interior, one of the most enduring themes in Ethiopian history is its relation to the Red Sea and through it the Mediterranean, Arabian and Asian worlds. Not only was the sea a major entry point for the arrival of imported goods, but it was an important cultural gateway as well. In this early period Ethiopia and Eritrea differed from Nubia, which was to a much greater degree oriented towards the Nile and Egypt. To be sure, traders certainly shipped goods along the Nile and then unloaded them for further shipment at Red Sea harbours. Access to India was important in most periods, and not surprisingly the Red Sea has been labelled 'a sea on the way to somewhere else'.[15]

Given that Aksum is located about 300 kilometres (186 mi.) from the coast (early sources say the journey took between five and fifteen days), one of the important questions is its precise relationship with the port city of Adulis. Although we often read that Aksumite domination of the port of Adulis was a major factor in the rise of the state, it could just as easily be true that Aksumite access to resources in the interior led to its eventual dominance of coastal trade. A crucial element of Aksumite power was its ability to secure the trade routes in the interior. The fourth-century ruler 'Ezana is said to have conducted a punitive raid against outsiders who attacked his trade routes within northeast Africa: 'When Tsarame, whose country is Afan, attacked and annihilated a merchant caravan . . . [therefore] we went to war against them.'[16]

In the past decades, the question of the relationship between Aksum and Adulis has gained additional attention, as it is coloured by contemporary issues of Ethiopian–Eritrean politics. According to some, a Pre-Aksumite independent Adulis foreshadowed Eritrean self-definition, while others view Aksumite rule of Adulis as evidence of Ethiopian sovereignty over the area.

While the emergence of Adulis may pre-date that of Aksum, it appears likely that it reached its peak only centuries later.[17] Adulis was continuously inhabited from the first or second century BCE to the sixth or early seventh century CE and was at its zenith in the fifth and sixth centuries.[18] Pottery imported from the highlands seems to be more abundant in the fifth and sixth centuries than in the earlier periods, which may be a sign of greater Aksumite influence during this period.

Of special value for an understanding of the early history of Adulis and the Red Sea is a unique document in Greek known as *The Periplus of the Erythraean Sea* (*periplus* meaning 'sailing around').[19] This anonymous first-century CE trading guide offers information about the monsoon winds, trade routes and, perhaps most importantly, the products that can be imported to or exported from harbours along the 'Erythraean Sea', which included the Red Sea, the Persian Gulf and the Indian Ocean. It reports that among the items available at Adulis were tortoise-shell, hides, ivory and slaves. It also notes that the local ruler, Zoscales, knew Greek.

Although Adulis is commonly referred to as a port, the *Periplus* tells us (and recent research confirms) that it was located 20 stadia (3.2 km/2 mi.) from the sea. (The distance has changed a little over the centuries due to silting.) This is a result of the existence of dual towns: one dedicated to locals and administration (Adulis) and a second (Gäbäza) which was on the coast and served as a customs post and housed the merchants. In this manner the political centre was 'protected' not only from pirates, 'Barbaroi dwelling roundabout', but from the cultural and political influence of foreigners.[20] (A well-known African example of this phenomenon was in ancient Ghana, where traders were confined to a different town from the ruler and locals.)

It is important to note at this point that beginning in the second half of the second century CE there was also a notable Aksumite presence on the other side of the Red Sea. Several Sabean inscriptions mention Abyssinians (Ḥabšat), who in alliance with local populations engaged in armed conflict with South Arabian rulers. I return to this theme later.[21]

Yet another vital early source for the history of Aksum and Adulis is a much later travelogue known as the 'Christian Topography' and attributed to an anonymous traveller who has become known as Cosmas Indicopleustes ('who sailed to India').[22] Although Cosmas was in the area of Adulis circa 518, which as we shall see in the next chapter was a crucial period, much of the importance of his report rests on a copy that he made of a far earlier inscription on a throne.

Glen Bowersock has recently argued convincingly that this inscription should be dated to the first decades of the third century CE and attributed to an Aksumite king. In this text, known as *Monumentum Adulitanum*, the king boasts of his successes throughout the highlands, towards the coast, north towards Meroë and even across the sea into South Arabia. He wrote during

Sketch reconstruction by Daniel Krencker from 1906 of the Throne of Adulis with inscriptions.

the period of an Aksumite occupation of part of South Arabia, which ended with the Aksumite withdrawal circa 270. As Bowersock notes with perhaps a little exaggeration, 'This extraordinary document marks the beginning of our knowledge of the kingdom of Axum.'[23]

Stelae

The most remarkable visual markers of early northern Ethiopian–Eritrean culture are the stelae erected in the area in and around Aksum. As I shall discuss below, this is not the last time that the region's most durable monuments were literally cut in stone. While these were at one time believed to be yet another Semitic/South Arabian import to northeast Africa, their local roots have been convincingly demonstrated.

For more than a century, archaeological teams of various nationalities have carried out intensive excavations in Aksum and the nearby hilltop of Betä Giyorgis, which overlooks the city. Residential areas, inscriptions, quarries and grave sites have been uncovered.

Many stelae were quarried about 4 kilometres (2½ mi.) from Aksum and then transported to the city. Since archaeologists have located several of these quarries, and even identified stelae that were begun but not completed, it is relatively easy to reconstruct the process from excavation to erection. This was a remarkable feat of engineering, human organization and animal (elephant) labour. The production of the stelae required several stages of stone cutting, including freeing the rock from the base rock, shaping it and, while it was still prone, carving designs into it. Given the

Stelae field in Aksum.

Reverse of Ethiopian 100 birr banknote with an illustration of the 'Rome' stela (the Aksum Obelisk) above the final digit 0.

intricacies of these engravings, they must have been made by teams who worked simultaneously side by side under supervisors who assured timely work and uniform production. Several stelae were decorated in the form of multistorey buildings. The erection of the stelae required the use of ropes or chains and pulleys and was a tremendous physical challenge. The largest stela is about 30 metres (98 ft) long, weighs about 520 tonnes and is carved on all its surfaces of nepheline syenite.[24] It may never have been successfully erected.

Although there has been much speculation regarding their purpose, 'the only firmly attested function of the African stelae is a grave marker.'[25] Significantly, the most impressive are adjacent to often elaborate mausolea. Indeed, it must be understood that the entire process represented a remarkable expression of royal power and the ability to command resources.

The second-largest stela is 24 metres (79 ft) long and weighs about 150 tonnes. It was taken to Italy in 1937 at the command of the Italian Fascist leader Mussolini and erected in Rome. Although the Italians agreed to repatriate all stolen Ethiopian treasures in 1947, only after a long public campaign was the stela returned to Ethiopia in 2005 and re-erected in 2008.

Although these stelae are clearly a survival from Ethiopia's Aksumite past, we find echoes of their style centuries later, most notably in the churches of Lalibäla. It is, moreover, fascinating to see both imperial and post-imperial governments employ them as national symbols for much later generations. Images of the stelae highlighted the Ethiopian pavilions at the World's Fairs in Montreal (1967) and Hanover (2000) and appeared on the national currency.

Pre-Christian religion

Most of our knowledge of the pre-Christian religion of Aksum comes from royal inscriptions. Although it is tempting to associate the deities worshipped at Aksum with either Greek or South Arabian gods, neither of these lineages offers a completely satisfactory explanation for the entirety of the divinities represented.

Mədr and Bəḥer appear to be designations for the diety (deities?) who represented the earth. 'Astär, who seems to be a god of the sky, is the only Aksumite deity who also appears in South Arabian inscriptions. He appears as early as inscriptions from D'mt, and within the early (sixth-century) translations of the Bible into Gə'əz. Mäḥrəm/Ares is a dynastic deity strongly associated with the ruler. The king who erected the throne with the *Monumentum Adulitanum* inscription wrote of 'my great god Ares', and prior to his conversion to Christianity the fourth-century ruler 'Ezana called himself the 'son of Mäḥrəm'.

Based on the limited sources at our disposal it is difficult to reconstruct an Aksumite pantheon. Not only is there a lack of evidence, but even for the brief period in question the situation appears to have been fluid and dynamic. Over the course of time, Mäḥrəm appears to have supplanted Mədr and Bəḥer. The god 'Astär also shows an interesting development; at least some believers associated Astar with the divinity of Judaism and Christianity and the name appears as the translation for the name of God in the Ethiopic translation of the pre-Christian apocryphal Book of Sirach (Ecclesiasticus).[26]

As we saw in the previous chapter there are Ethiopian traditions which suggest that prior to the arrival of Christianity, traditional religions included the veneration of snakes. However, no material evidence exists in support of this claim. Similarly, despite traditions that much of the Ethiopian population adopted Judaism before Christianity, none of the existing archaeological evidence supports this claim.

Yet another important source for the reconstruction of early Aksumite history and religion are coins that were minted for about three hundred years from the end of the third century until about the middle of the seventh century.[27] Aksum was the only ancient sub-Saharan African kingdom to issue coins.[28] These coins are a much more reliable witness to the names of successive Aksumite rulers than the numerous king lists which were composed many years later. About twenty different rulers are attested to in these coins, of which only two ('Ezana and Kaleb) are also found in other contemporary sources. Prior to the acceptance of Christianity, crescents, stars and stalks appear as symbols of divine approbation.

To produce these coins Aksumite kings used large amounts of bronze and silver, as well as gold. The captions on the gold coins and most of the silver ones are in Greek. The choice of Greek was not with an eye to the circulation of Aksumite money in the Mediterranean basin, but primarily for the Red Sea trade. Hoards of gold Aksumite coins have been found in Aksum, Adulis, Arabia (present-day Yemen) and India. The silver and copper coins are primarily represented by strays found in northern Ethiopia and may have been designed for local use.

THREE
A CHRISTIAN KINGDOM

The introduction of Christianity to the kingdom of Aksum was one of the most important and impactful events in its history. There are several accounts that are cited to explain this early adoption, which was preceded only by Armenia and Rome.

The 'Ethiopian' eunuch of the New Testament

According to Ethiopian tradition, the arrival of Christianity can be traced to the earliest period of that faith. In the Acts of the Apostles (8:26–38) we read of an 'Ethiopian', a servant of the great queen Candace, who was converted by the Apostle Philip:

> **26** And the angel of the Lord spake unto Philip, saying, Arise, and go toward the south unto the way that goeth down from Jerusalem unto Gaza, which is desert.
> **27** And he arose and went: and, behold, a man of Ethiopia, an eunuch of great authority under Candace queen of the Ethiopians, who had the charge of all her treasure, and had come to Jerusalem for to worship,
> **28** Was returning, and sitting in his chariot read Esaias the prophet.
> **29** Then the Spirit said unto Philip, Go near, and join thyself to this chariot.
> **30** And Philip ran thither to him, and heard him read the prophet Esaias, and said, Understandest thou what thou readest?

31 And he said, How can I, except some man should guide me?
And he desired Philip that he would come up and sit with him.
32 The place of the scripture which he read was this, He was
led as a sheep to the slaughter; and like a lamb dumb before
his shearer, so opened he not his mouth:
33 In his humiliation his judgment was taken away: and who
shall declare his generation? for his life is taken from the earth.
34 And the eunuch answered Philip, and said, I pray thee, of
whom speaketh the prophet this? of himself, or of some other
man?
35 Then Philip opened his mouth, and began at the same
scripture, and preached unto him Jesus.
36 And as they went on their way, they came unto a certain
water: and the eunuch said, See, here is water; what doth
hinder me to be baptized?
37 And Philip said, If thou believest with all thine heart, thou
mayest. And he answered and said, I believe that Jesus Christ
is the Son of God.
38 And he commanded the chariot to stand still: and they
went down both into the water, both Philip and the eunuch;
and he baptized him.

This short passage has been subject to considerable discussion and interpretation. Several Church Fathers contrast the Blackness of the eunuch with the presumed whiteness of his converted soul, and even use the story to affirmatively answer Jeremiah's question (Jeremiah 13:23) 'Can the Ethiopian change his skin . . .?' Others go beyond the text to claim that after these events he returned home and evangelized Ethiopia.

There has also been a great deal of speculation about the pre-conversion religious identity of the 'eunuch'. Was he a Jew, a Gentile or somewhere in between? Some compare him to Ebed-Melech (lit. 'the Servant/Slave of the King'), mentioned in Jeremiah 38, who is also identified as an Ethiopian, and saved the prophet when he was cast into a cistern. Many perceive it as noteworthy that at an early date the Church did not accept racial distinctions. More recently, some modern theologians have cited the eunuch as an early example of Christianity's tolerance of sexual minorities.

Despite the Ethiopian Christian attachment to this story in recent years, scholars are in general agreement that it does not refer to the Aksumite kingdom, but rather to the Nubian kingdom of Meroë. As I discussed in the Prologue to this volume the Greek term *aithiops* does not denote either modern Ethiopia or the highland peoples who were the ancestors of the present-day inhabitants of the Ethiopian plateau. In the case of this episode the use of the name Candace almost certainly refers to the *kandake* (queen mother) in the ancient Nubian kingdom of Meroë.

Certainly, there were ample incentives for Christian Ethiopians to identify themselves with this early Apostolic-age conversion and thus highlight the antiquity of their Christianity. The eunuch's conversion is commemorated by the Ethiopian Church. However, we do not have any source that records the tradition as referring to an Aksumite prior to the arrival of the Portuguese in Ethiopia.[1] Moreover, the conversion of the eunuch is not depicted in any pre-modern Ethiopian church or in Ethiopian manuscript illumination.[2]

Frumentius and Aedesius

Yet another story, which appears in a variety of sources, connects us more closely to a specific historical event. Arriving in 'Further India' as refugees from a plundered ship on the Red Sea coast, two Syrian brothers were taken as captives to the court of the king. One of them, Aedesius, was made the king's cup-bearer, while the other, Frumentius, became his treasurer and secretary. When the monarch died, his queen asked them to serve as regents until her infant son was old enough to rule the kingdom himself. During this period, Frumentius took advantage of his position to seek out and support the Christian merchants residing in the kingdom. When the prince had grown up and assumed the throne, the two Syrians left India. Aedesius returned home to Tyre, and Frumentius travelled to Alexandria, where he met the bishop, Athanasius I. Apprised of the situation, where the local Christians lacked clergy, Athanasius appointed Frumentius as the first bishop to Ethiopia. Frumentius then returned to Aksum and preached Christianity throughout the kingdom.

> Now, when the royal child whose kingdom they had looked after reached maturity, then, having executed their trust completely and handed it back faithfully, they returned to our continent, even though the queen and her son tried very hard to hold them back and asked them to stay. While Aedesius hastened to Tyre to see his parents and relatives again, Frumentius journeyed to Alexandria, saying that it was not right to conceal what the Lord had done. He therefore explained to the bishop everything that had been done and urged him to provide some worthy man to send as bishop to the already numerous Christians and churches built on barbarian soil. Then Athanasius, for he had recently received the priesthood, after considering attentively and carefully what Frumentius had said and done, spoke as follows in the council of priests: 'What other man can we find like you, in whom is God's spirit as in you, and who could achieve such things as these?' And having conferred on him the priesthood, he ordered him to return with the Lord's grace to the place from which he had come. When he had reached India as bishop, it is said that such a grace of miracles was given him by God that the signs of the Apostles were worked by him and a countless number of barbarians was converted to the faith. From that time on there came into existence a Christian people and churches in India, and the priesthood began. These events we came to know of not from popular rumour, but from the report of Aedesius himself, who had been Frumentius's companion, and who later became a presbyter in Tyre.[3]

India?

Obviously one of the features of this narrative which must be clarified is the use of the term 'India'. A variety of terms were used to refer to the region of northeast Africa. We saw in the Prologue the ambiguity regarding the use of the terms 'Ethiopia' and 'India'. Certainly, the latter often designated the basin of the Indus river.[4] However, over the course of time and through the division of the distant areas into three separate realms, Greater India, Lesser India and Middle India, the terms were used to reference a series of locations, including not only the Indian subcontinent and the areas of the Indus valley but such Red Sea countries as South Arabia, Somalia and Ethiopia. Although at a very early stage (the second century BCE or earlier) ancient authors were aware of the distinction between India, Arabia and Ethiopia, the use of the designation 'India' for areas outside the subcontinent proved remarkably durable.

It should also be noted that there is rich evidence for trade links between the subcontinent and northeast Africa, including the exchange of pepper, precious stones, ivory and other animal products. However, in contrast to the story of the Ethiopian eunuch, there is no question that the story of Frumentius deals not with the subcontinent but with the area of the Aksumite kingdom.

For all its legendary character, the main outlines of this story are confirmed by a variety of sources.[5] In 356/7 the Roman emperor Constantius II (r. 337–61) wrote to the Aksumite rulers Aeizana(s) ('Ezana) and Sazana(s) explaining that because the Egyptian Church leader, Athanasius of Alexandria, was a heretic (an opponent of the theologian Arius) his consecration was not valid and therefore he should return to Egypt for a proper consecration by the Arian archbishop, George of Cappadocia.[6] We have no idea if the Ethiopians received this letter. Certainly, there is no evidence that they acted on it.

In circa 330–65, the kingdom of Aksum was ruled by one of its most famous rulers, 'Ezana, who is commemorated in gold, silver and copper coins, about a dozen inscriptions and literary sources in several languages. Coins from early in 'Ezana's reign bear his image and name, and on the other side the symbol of the crescent moon. Those from later periods bear a cross.

In 'Ezana's earlier inscriptions he dedicates his victories in war to several of the gods worshipped in the Aksumite religious world. He refers to himself as 'the son of Mäḥrəm, who cannot be conquered by the enemy'.[7] Other divinities he invoked included Astar and the indigenous divinities Bəḥer and Mədr.

In one later inscription he invokes the 'Lord of Heaven'.[8] This monotheistic 'Lord of Heaven' inscription was discovered by 1906 as part of the Deutsche Aksum-Expedition led by the German orientalist Enno Littmann. For many years scholars debated the significance of this text, claiming that 'Ezana had become a Jew, or a Judaized monotheist, or a generic monotheist, or a Christian.[9] Only in 1970 was an unambiguously Christian inscription published.[10] It reads:

> In faith in God and in the power of the Father and the Son and the Holy Spirit, in the one
> Who saved the kingdom for me in the faith of his Son Jesus Christ, who helped me
> And who always helps me, I 'Ezana, king of the Aksumites and the Ḥimyarites, of Raydan, of the Sabaeans, Ṣalḥen, of Kasu, Bəga,
> Servant of Christ, thank the Lord my God, And has given me great name through his Son,
> In whom I have believed, and for me he makes him
> Leader of my whole kingdom on the basis

Christian Aksumite coin, 4th or 5th century, silver alloy.

Faith in Christ according to his will and
Through the power of Christ . . . indefatigable.[11]

To this day scholars debate whether the difference between the monotheistic and Christian inscriptions is social (local polytheists versus Graeco-Egyptian merchants) or chronological; an evolution from animism to monotheism to Christianity.[12] However, there can be little question that ʿEzana is signalling a religious change.

We should be wary about overestimating the immediate impact of ʿEzana's conversion. While the ruler clearly declared himself to be a Christian, at least in Greek for the purposes of presentation to Aksum's foreign traders and some other residents, most of the population had not converted and were probably unaffected by his decision. Moreover, until the Bible had been translated into Gəʿəz and a sufficient number of clergy consecrated, the Church had certain obvious limitations.

Nevertheless, we now have clear evidence that early Aksumite Christianity was not merely a court religion. About 6 or so kilometres (4 mi.) northeast of Yəḥa is Betä Sämati, where archaeological excavations have produced major discoveries since 2010. Just the continued occupation of the site puts paid to the claim that the Yəḥa region was abandoned during the Aksumite Period. In fact, Betä Sämati was an administrative centre from the eighth century BCE to the seventh century CE. Throughout this period it continued to serve as a station on the trade route from the coast to Aksum. It was also one of the earliest Christian towns, as is confirmed by an ancient basilica with a Gəʿəz inscription reading 'for this entrance, Christ be favourable to us.'[13] Moreover, in keeping with the complexity found in ʿEzana's inscriptions, the Betä Sämati basilica demonstrates a mix of religious and secular functions (stamp seals and tokens which may have been used for calculations) and 'pagan' (figurines and ceramic ornaments) as well as the obviously Christian objects, including crosses.

It is important to note that ʿEzana's reign was also the occasion for another important cultural innovation. For the first time the local literary language, Gə'əz, was written with vocalization. To this day, Gə'əz is the only Semitic language that represents

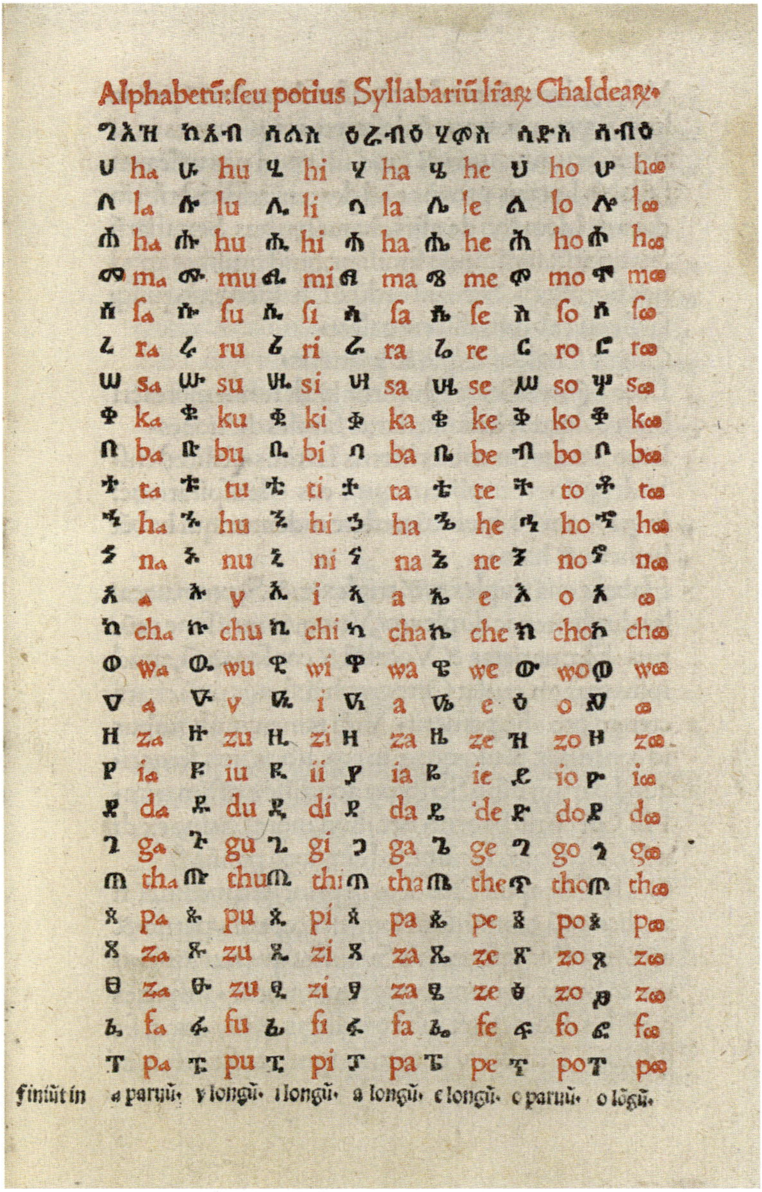

Alphabetũ: ſeu potius Syllabariũ lrãꝝ Chaldeaꝝ.

ግእዝ		ካእብ		ሣልስ		ራብዕ		ኃምስ		ሳድስ		ሳብዕ	
ሀ	ha	ሁ	hu	ሂ	hi	ሃ	ha	ሄ	he	ህ	ho	ሆ	hω
ለ	la	ሉ	lu	ሊ	li	ላ	la	ሌ	le	ል	lo	ሎ	lω
ሐ	ha	ሑ	hu	ሒ	hi	ሓ	ha	ሔ	he	ሕ	ho	ሖ	hω
መ	ma	ሙ	mu	ሚ	mi	ማ	ma	ሜ	me	ም	mo	ሞ	mω
ሠ	ſa	ሡ	ſu	ሢ	ſi	ሣ	ſa	ሤ	ſe	ሥ	ſo	ሦ	ſω
ረ	ra	ሩ	ru	ሪ	ri	ራ	ra	ሬ	re	ር	ro	ሮ	rω
ሰ	sa	ሱ	su	ሲ	si	ሳ	sa	ሴ	se	ስ	so	ሶ	sω
ቀ	ka	ቁ	ku	ቂ	ki	ቃ	ka	ቄ	ke	ቅ	ko	ቆ	kω
በ	ba	ቡ	bu	ቢ	bi	ባ	ba	ቤ	be	ብ	bo	ቦ	bω
ተ	ta	ቱ	tu	ቲ	ti	ታ	ta	ቴ	te	ት	to	ቶ	tω
ኀ	ha	ኁ	hu	ኂ	hi	ኃ	ha	ኄ	he	ኅ	ho	ኆ	hω
ነ	na	ኑ	nu	ኒ	ni	ና	na	ኔ	ne	ን	no	ኖ	nω
አ	a	ኡ	v	ኢ	i	ኣ	a	ኤ	e	እ	o	ኦ	ω
ከ	cha	ኩ	chu	ኪ	chi	ካ	cha	ኬ	che	ክ	cho	ኮ	chω
ወ	wa	ዉ	wu	ዊ	wi	ዋ	wa	ዌ	we	ው	wo	ዎ	wω
ዐ	a	ዑ	v	ዒ	i	ዓ	a	ዔ	e	ዕ	o	ዖ	ω
ዘ	za	ዙ	zu	ዚ	zi	ዛ	za	ዜ	ze	ዝ	zo	ዞ	zω
የ	ia	ዩ	iu	ዪ	ii	ያ	ia	ዬ	ie	ይ	io	ዮ	iω
ደ	da	ዱ	du	ዲ	di	ዳ	da	ዴ	de	ድ	do	ዶ	dω
ገ	ga	ጉ	gu	ጊ	gi	ጋ	ga	ጌ	ge	ግ	go	ጎ	gω
ጠ	tha	ጡ	thu	ጢ	thi	ጣ	tha	ጤ	the	ጥ	tho	ጦ	thω
ጰ	pa	ጱ	pu	ጲ	pi	ጳ	pa	ጴ	pe	ጵ	po	ጶ	pω
ጸ	za	ጹ	zu	ጺ	zi	ጻ	za	ጼ	ze	ጽ	zo	ጾ	zω
ፀ	za	ፁ	zu	ፂ	zi	ፃ	za	ፄ	ze	ፅ	zo	ፆ	zω
ፈ	fa	ፉ	fu	ፊ	fi	ፋ	fa	ፌ	fe	ፍ	fo	ፎ	fω
ፐ	pa	ፑ	pu	ፒ	pi	ፓ	pa	ፔ	pe	ፕ	po	ፖ	pω
finiũt in	a paruũ		v longũ		i longũ		a longũ		e longũ		e paruũ		o lõgũ

Ethiopic syllabary, from the Ethiopic Psalter of 1513, entitled *Psalterium David et cantica aliqua in lingua Chaldea*.

Mural painting of Frumentius (Abunä Sälama I), 17th century.

vocalization not by separate vowel signs above or below the line, but rather by a relatively systematic modification of the letters themselves. Thus while traditional Hebrew is written with vocalization under the letters and Eastern Syriac was written with vowel indications above and below letters, Gəʾəz and later other Semitic languages of Ethiopia were vocalized through changes in the shape of letters.

This system of vocalization, known as abugida or alphasyllabary, is comparatively rare but is widespread in the Indian subcontinent. Some scholars believe the use of this form to be the result of Indian influence and specifically the impact of Brahmi script. In the year 2000 archaeological excavations in a cave called Ḥōq on the island of Socotra in the Indian Ocean found inscriptions using Indian script (many), South Arabian (ten), Greek (four) and Gəʾəz (ten). Although only three of this last group that can be deciphered are clearly Christian in character and hence cannot date from earlier than the fourth century (and are probably later), the overlap is suggestive.[14] Similarly enticing but not definitive is the discovery, too, of Aksumite coins from the first half of the fourth century in India.[15] The different peoples of northern Ethiopia – by accepting Christianity and developing their own literary language – created for themselves the basis on which they founded their own nation. Certainly, a vocalized script would have made reading, whether for personal use or aloud to a community, easier for the small part of the population that was literate.

A foreign leader for a national Church

The appointment of Frumentius as the first leader of the Church in Ethiopia is invoked as a precedent which lasted for 1,600 years. Until the middle of the twentieth century, the *de jure* head of the Ethiopian Church was a monk chosen by the patriarch of the Church in Egypt, which came to be known as the Coptic Church.[16] While the modern reader might assume that the Ethiopians could at any time have shrugged off the Egyptian dominance, this was not, in fact, the case. To claim an unbroken link to Christ and his apostles, the Ethiopians needed to establish an alternative direct connection to the Apostles. While they could have gone outside Egypt (to Syria, for example) and they appear to have attempted this at various times, this was not easily done for both geographical and political reasons.

After the Muslim conquest of Egypt (639–42), Egypt was a Muslim-ruled country. (Even though the Copts probably only became a minority population after a few centuries.) Thus the patriarch of the Coptic Church could only approve the Ethiopian request with the consent of the Muslim ruler of Egypt. For a variety of reasons, the monks sent from Egypt were not always of the highest quality. Being 'kicked upstairs', or in this case 'up the river' to Ethiopia, was a convenient way to rid Egypt of a troublesome cleric. While some metropolitans, heads of the 'diocese' of Ethiopia, were outstanding leaders, others were less suited to the task. The ninth-century Abuna Yuhanna (John) is said to have arrived without having been circumcised. When the locals objected, he agreed to undergo the ritual rather than face the dangerous journey back to Egypt. However, on the fateful day he was revealed to have been miraculously circumcised and thus was spared the ritual.[17] In the early twelfth century a monk named George was sent to Ethiopia but acted so disgracefully that the Ethiopian king arrested him and sent him back to Egypt. There he was imprisoned because 'he transgressed . . . in infamous affairs and in vile deeds'.[18] Later in that century another metropolitan was sent back to Egypt because of his extravagant style and for allegedly murdering a priest.[19]

Even the best-qualified appointees had to be aware that their co-religionists in Egypt would probably suffer if the Muslims of Ethiopia were persecuted or harmed. Moreover, with few exceptions these Egyptian clerics did not know the languages of Ethiopia, either spoken (Amharic/Təgrəñña) or ecclesiastical (Gəʿəz), and thus their communication and liturgical powers were limited. (I discuss notable exceptions such as Abunä Sälama II, known as 'the Translator', in Chapter Seven and also consider how nineteenth- and twentieth-century tensions regarding this arrangement may have influenced scholarly perceptions.)

The Coptic Church also differed theologically but especially ritually from its Ethiopian 'daughter'. Thus the Saturday Sabbath of the Ethiopians was anathema to many Egyptians and at times (particularly in the fourteenth and fifteenth centuries) this created major tensions between the abun (metropolitan, lit. 'father'), his allies and large parts of the Church. Circumcision appears to be another custom on which the two Churches differed.

Despite all these drawbacks the abun was crucial to the survival of the Church in Ethiopia. Only he was qualified to consecrate clergy: priests and deacons. The combination of the perils of the journey from Ethiopia to Egypt and back, and the difficulties of negotiating with the reigning ruler through the Coptic patriarch, resulted in long periods when there was no abun.

In the absence of a metropolitan, the older clergy gradually died off and the Church declined. Only the priests, after all, could perform the sacraments: baptism, confirmation, communion, marriage, confession and penance, unction for the sick. One solution was to consecrate as many priests and deacons as possible when a metropolitan was available. And the Portuguese reported in the sixteenth century on mass consecrations in which candidates were lined up and certified with only the most minimal concern for their learning or other qualifications.[20]

Throughout much of Ethiopian history the emperor was the de facto head of the Church. While formally his status was no different from any other Christian believer, his political power, military prowess and control of economic resources, especially land, all gave him tremendous influence in the life of the Church. The abun, like the pope, had no divisions.

While it is easy in retrospect to see patterns which were established in the fourth century and continued throughout Ethiopian Christian history, it is important not to exaggerate the impact of 'Ezana's conversion. As the ambiguity of his inscriptions and coins indicates, only a small portion of the population were immediately affected by or even aware of the change. It is worth making a distinction between the conversion of the king to Christianity and the 'Christianization' of the kingdom: the adoption of Christianity as the basis for the organizing principles of the kingdom.[21]

Although he is remembered best for his conversion, we should not overlook other aspects of 'Ezana's reign. Like his predecessors and successors, he left inscriptions in several languages commemorating his victories over local rivals. These not only testify to his religious orientation, but help us document his campaigns against the Beğa (Bega), Noba (Nubia) and Kasu (Kush) (that is, Meroë). Although Aksum did not exercise political sovereignty over any part of South Arabia at this time, significantly he continued to style himself as the ruler of Ḥimyar! I discuss the consequences of this irredentism/political mythology in the next chapter.

FOUR
The Development of the Church and the Arrival of Islam

During the almost two centuries after 'Ezana's conversion, Christianity became firmly established in the Aksumite kingdom. Written sources and epigraphy indicate that this new religion took root in the early fourth century but its adoption by a wider population was a gradual process.[1]

We have only limited reliable information regarding the development of Christianity in Ethiopia in the wake of 'Ezana's conversion. Ethiopian tradition records that in the late fifth and early sixth centuries foreign missionaries reached Ethiopia and helped consolidate the presence of Christianity. Known as the Ṣadəqan (the Righteous Ones) and the Nine Saints, they are credited with the introduction of monasticism as well as the translation of the Bible into Gəʿəz.

The association of these missionaries with Syriac-speaking areas (Syriac was the main literary language of Aramaic-speaking Christians in the area east of the Mediterranean) was accepted for many years but has been seriously challenged in most recent scholarship. Most of their personal names and the geographical names of their places of origin do not appear to be of Syriac origin.[2] Similarly, the claim that the Bible was translated from Syriac into Gəʿəz has been debunked. Moreover, several recent studies have cast considerable doubt on how much information can be drawn from the hagiographies of these saints, which were written centuries after the events they claim to record.[3] Scholars increasingly view their hagiographies as providing 'much later interpretations of the facts, transmitted through a medieval cultural background'.[4] Although

Early Ethiopian monastic saints depicted in a 17th-century cloth mural, Däbrä Sina.

the *Gädlä Ṗantälewon* (Life of Ṗantälewon) was composed in the fourteenth century, and that of Abba Gärima (see below) in the fifteenth, most of these works are much later – perhaps even from the nineteenth and twentieth centuries!

These historical challenges notwithstanding, there can be little doubt that, during the decades after ʿEzana, Christianity consolidated its position within the Aksumite kingdom. Whatever the process may have been, and whoever the specific agents of change were, there is firm evidence that a local clergy, including monks, emerged, that scriptures were translated, and that Christianity spread beyond the confines of Aksum and the court.

Obviously, the translation of Scripture into the local language was a necessity if the religion was to spread among the masses. This is not, of course, to claim that more than a tiny fraction of the population of Aksum were literate and able to read religious texts. Moreover, given the technical difficulties and heavy expenses involved in hand-copying texts onto hard-to-acquire parchments, the number of manuscripts must have also been extremely limited. Nevertheless, this was a crucial process and perhaps most importantly required a partnership between local believers, with their expertise in Gəʿəz, and foreigners familiar with the intricacies of the Greek text.

Until recently, it was thought that no documents from this ancient period had survived. However, two manuscripts – known as the Gärima Gospels because they come from the ancient Təgrean monastery of Abba Gärima, near the historic city of Adwa – are said to have been written by the eponymous monk who founded that community. Although these manuscripts were long thought to date at the earliest to the tenth or eleventh century, many authors now assign them to 530–660 (Gärima 1)

Cupola of the Nine Saints, Abuna Yemata Guh, 15th century. Only eight of the saints are depicted in this cupola, with Abuna Yemata being depicted on the wall.

and 390–570 (Gärima 2). This makes them not only the oldest surviving Gəʿəz manuscripts, but among the oldest extant illustrated Christian Gospel manuscripts in the world.[5]

Unfortunately, we do not have any witness of similar antiquity for the text of the Old Testament (Hebrew Bible) or later works such as Enoch, Jubilees, the Ascension of Isaiah, Rest of the Words of Baruch or 4 Baruch, and the Third and Fourth Book of Ezra, which are not accepted as canonical by many Churches but are viewed as such by the Ethiopian Orthodox Church. The best we can do are short excerpts from biblical texts found in inscriptions in Ethiopia and South Arabia. Almost all our Old Testament manuscripts date from the fourteenth century and later.[6]

Although the Bible was undoubtedly the most important of the works translated from Greek during the Aksumite Period, it was not the only project of this kind. Among the other works that were probably translated were several with a specifically Egyptian flavour: two versions of the monastic rules of the Egyptian monk Pachomius, which played a major role in shaping Ethiopian monasticism; the Life of St Antony, which is attributed to St Athanasius; a version of the Acts of St Mark, who was martyred in Alexandria; the Life of St Paul of Thebes; and the Qerəllos, a collection of theological treatises by various Church leaders, including Cyril of Alexandria.

Special mention must be made of what is known as the 'Aksumite Collection': a unique canonical–liturgical compilation found only in a single thirteenth-century manuscript. It preserves a set of translations from Greek to Gəʾəz which can be dated to sometime between the fifth and seventh centuries. Among the important works it contains are a portion of the *History of the Episcopate of Alexandria*, an archaic version of the *Apostolic Tradition*, a *Baptismal Order*, a *Euchologion* (an important liturgical text), letters of the anti-Chalcedonian patriarch Timotheus Aelurus (d. 477) and a treatise *Concerning the Only Judge*.[7]

Unfortunately, we are unable to say with any certainty how long the Ethiopian Church or its Egyptian leadership retained a knowledge of Greek and used it as a source for translation. It appears unlikely that the Greek influence survived for long after the Muslim conquest of Egypt in the first half of the seventh century. The scholarly consensus is that most if not all Gəʿəz works translated directly from the Greek should be dated during or shortly after the Aksumite Period.

Monasticism

The early history of churches, monasteries and monasticism in Ethiopia is also difficult to reconstruct. Some of the earliest monasteries were built over the sites of ancient temples. One of the oldest monasteries in the country is Däbrä Dammo, which is located on a flat-topped mountain (*amba*) near Adwa in Təgray.[8] Tradition (his *gädl*, or *vita*, dates from the sixteenth century) tells us that the monastery's founder, Abba ZäMikaʾel Arägawi, climbed the tail of a great snake in order to ascend to the top of the site. To this day access to Däbrä Dammo is possible only via ropes which are lowered almost 15 metres (50 ft) so devotees can reach the monastery. According to his *gädl* he was accompanied into Ethiopia by his mother, who is credited with establishing the first nunnery in the country.

Although the inaccessibility of the site offered it a certain protection, it has been destroyed and rebuilt several times since its founding. It appears to have been spared during the Muslim conquest of Ethiopia in the first half of the sixteenth century, but it fell victim to Turkish forces a few years later in 1557. At one time the monastery housed a large collection of valuable manuscripts (the monks claimed over a thousand), but a fire in 2014 appears to have destroyed many of these. More recently, in early 2021, during fighting between Təgrayan rebels and Eritrean forces allied with the central Ethiopian government, there were eyewitness reports of conflicts in the area, including the shelling and destruction of parts of the monastery and allegations of looting of many of its valuables.[9]

According to the traditions of the Nine Saints, a century or so after this Abba Afṣe built a church and monastery in Yəḥa, which we have seen had Sabean and early Aksumite cultic reverberations. It should also be noted that recent excavations in Adulis of two churches in the city indicate that they were first built in the fifth

Ascending to the Monastery of Däbrä Dammo.

or even as late as the early sixth century.[10] Thus in the decades and centuries after ‘Ezana's conversion, Christianity became an increasingly important part of the countryside's visual culture.

There is a third feature of the development of Ethiopian Christianity that can also be traced to the centuries after ‘Ezana's conversion. As has been discussed in detail, during its first centuries, and particularly after the conversion of the Roman emperor

Constantine, there were deep controversies within Christianity regarding the nature of Christ. In 451, at the Council of Chalcedon, a major split took place between those who viewed Christ as having 'one person in two natures', who were called Dyophysites, and those including the Copts, Syrian Orthodox, Armenians and Ethiopians, who argued for one single nature of Christ after the union of divinity and humanity.

The Ethiopian Christians were not represented at Chalcedon and the terms for these divisions probably only came into wide currency several centuries later. Nevertheless, because of its connection to the Coptic Church and perhaps through the influence of the early monks discussed above, Ethiopian Christians have been widely seen as Monophysites.

It must be stressed that representatives of Eastern Orthodox churches, including the Ethiopians, reject this identification. Rather, they contend that the single nature of Christ is complex and that within that single nature, divinity and humanity are united without confusion or diminution. Accordingly, they prefer to be referred to as anti-Chalcedonians or more frequently Miaphysites. The official name of the Churches today is the Ethiopian/Eritrean Orthodox Täwaḥedo (united in one) Churches.

It must be stressed that although there is little question as to which 'camp' the Ethiopians belong, throughout their early history this was not the subject of violent controversies or theological disputes. While the Ethiopians were firm in their rejection of Chalcedon, their own position was not the subject of detailed articulation. As I discuss in Chapter Six, there were significant divisions that arose within the Church and particularly between its monastic movements from the fourteenth century on. These, however, were not focused on Christological matters until sometime later.

Kaleb

The next great ruler of Aksum was Kaleb (an Old Testament name!), or as he was also known Ǝlla Aṣbəḥa, who ruled in the first half of the sixth century. His reign is commemorated in inscriptions, coins and literary sources in several languages. He is credited with important innovations regarding the integration of Christianity into the political fabric of the Aksumite kingdom. According to some sources he was the first Aksumite ruler to be enthroned in a Christian ceremony.

Among the most interesting traditions (from centuries later) about Kaleb are those that associate him with the construction of the metropolitan cathedral of Aksum Ṣeyon. God is said to have revealed the location for this great church to the emperor by divine intervention at a site called Məkyadä Ǝgzi'ənä ('the footprint of our Lord'). The church itself is rich with symbolism invoking the church of Mount Zion in Jerusalem, which was the site of the Last Supper. Its ark (*tabot*) is dedicated to the Virgin Mary.

The original cathedral has been destroyed and rebuilt several times and what we see today owes much to the Gondarine Period of the seventeenth and eighteenth centuries. An adjacent building quite recently constructed is said to hold the Ark of the Covenant given to Moses and brought to Ethiopia by Israelites who accompanied Mənəlik I.

Kaleb is best known to the wider world for his conflict with Ḥimyar in South Arabia in 525.[11] Although 'Ezana is justly remembered as the first Christian ruler of Aksum, it is difficult to overestimate Kaleb's reputation for consolidating Christianity as a key element in Aksumite identity. Certainly, his reign marks the clear establishment of Christianity as a national faith with explicit political implications.

In the third century the rulers of Aksum exercised control over some areas of South Arabia. Even after these rulers had been decisively expelled from the region, later Aksumite rulers such as 'Ezana were confirmed irredentists and styled themselves as rulers not only of Aksumites and Ethiopians (Nubia?) but of Ḥimyarites and Sabaens.[12]

Kaleb shared with 'Ezana not only his Christian devotion, but a vision of himself as the ruler of both sides of the Red Sea. Already in 518 he had attempted to make this a reality by invading the country and placing a local Christian on the throne as his representative. At the same time the Judaized rulers of Ḥimyar also claimed to be the kings of some of the same territory and claimed links with the Queen of the South (the Queen of Sheba!). Thus on both sides of the Red Sea, rival rulers – one Jewish, one Christian – proclaimed their imperial visions in their inscriptions. Traders must have communicated these conflicting visions to both sides as they travelled back and forth between the two coasts of the Red Sea.

Kaleb's initial intervention was not intended to change the political order on a grand scale, but primarily to strengthen the Christian presence in the area. In an inscription celebrating his successes he proudly declared, 'I built a shrine at Himyar . . . zealous for the name of the Son of God, in Whom I believe, and I built His Gabaz [shrine] and sanctified it by the power of God.'[13] Eventually this led to war.

Kaleb appointed a local representative (probably a Christian) to represent Aksumite interests in the area, but when this governor died the position went to a local named Joseph (Yūsuf As'ar Yaṯ'ar), also known as Ḏū Nuwās. Shortly afterwards, in 522, Yūsuf rebelled. He destroyed the local churches and ravaged the Aksumite garrison in the capital, Ẓafar, massacring three hundred residents. After his victory, Ḏū Nuwās sought an alliance with the Sassanids in Iran, which would have blocked the important trade route from Egypt to India, via Ethiopia and Yemen, to Roman merchants. Most importantly, he sent troops against the oasis of Nağrän, where they met strong resistance. Eventually many Christians, all the Miaphysite community, were martyred. Indeed, Yūsuf appears to have boasted of his success in a letter in which he quoted freely from the anguished Christians' pleas for mercy. This provoked outrage across the Christian Orient.

In response to this atrocity, the Byzantine emperor Justin requested the intervention of the Aksumite ruler. Kaleb assumed the mantle of Christianity and with the support of the Roman fleet crossed the Red Sea in 525 and inflicted a devastating defeat on Ḏū Nuwās. After executing his rival, Kaleb set out to restore Aksumite sovereignty over the area and re-establish a Christian presence.

Despite his previous bad experience with indirect rule, Kaleb still did not change the political organization of the state. He once again placed a local representative on the Ḥimyarite throne. Moreover, Kaleb himself remained in Ḥimyar for a relatively short period before returning home. He left part of his army in Arabia to control the country and to guarantee the payment of an annual tribute. Ethiopian sources recount that Kaleb himself abdicated the throne upon his return and lived out the rest of his life as a hermit monk. While this may be as much a hagiographic topos as a historical event, several sites in Ethiopia commemorate this event to this day.

Numerous oral and written traditions associate Kaleb with the archaeological site of Endä Kaleb, about 2 kilometres (1¼ mi.) from the centre of Aksum. Two monumental tombs there are said to be those of Kaleb and his son Gäbrä Masqal. Not only are these mentioned in the fifteenth-century *Liber Axumae* (Book of Aksum), but they are described by numerous foreign travellers, including the sixteenth-century Portuguese chaplain Francisco Álvares and the nineteenth-century British explorer Henry Salt. While scholars agree that the site holds Aksumite remains, many believe they date to the period *before* Kaleb.

Once again Kaleb's implementation of indirect rule was not successful. Circa 535 (but perhaps as early as 531) a former slave named Abraha, who served as an officer in the Ethiopian army, deposed the ruler appointed by Kaleb. Repeated attempts to restore direct Aksumite control failed, although eventually Abraha agreed to pay tribute to Kaleb's successor.

Abraha greatly expanded the area under his control and built a cathedral at al-Qulays (Ṣanʿāʾ) whose mosaics, precious woods, gemstones and gold decorations rivalled both the grandeur of pre-Islamic Mecca and perhaps most significantly the great church of Maryam Ṣeyon in Aksum.[14] He also built numerous other churches, often more than one in a single city, such as Nağrān, Ẓafar and Akana. In one of his (Sabaen-language) inscriptions he identified himself as 'he who reveres the saviour, and king of Sabae' and is particularly proud of his support for repairs on the Great Märib dam, a massive structure built in the sixth century BCE which spanned more than 600 metres (1,970 ft) and helped irrigate an area of around 100 square kilometres (40 sq. mi.). It was

Tomb of Emperor Kaleb, Aksum.

at this site, in 548, that Abraha welcomed representatives from Aksum, Byzantium, (Sassanian) Persia and North Arabia, but significantly not the polytheistic Arabs who were his rivals.

Certainly, Abraha is best remembered in Muslim traditions for his attempt to conquer the important city of Mecca, which was already a centre of trade and pilgrimage. His ultimate failure in what is often referred to as the 'Year/Battle of the Elephant', because of the great beast he brought with his army, is traditionally associated with the birth of the Prophet Muhammed.[15] He and his troops are said to have been defeated by divine intervention, whether by a plague or being pelted from above by small stones. Scholars have long debated the historicity of these events and their dates, with some placing it as early as 552 and others almost two decades later. In part, at least, this appears to be related to the controversy as to whether the claim that Muhammed was forty years old when he was called to prophecy is a fact or a literary topos.

After Abraha's death (around 565?), his sons briefly succeeded him on Ḥimyar's throne. Shortly thereafter, Aksumite control over parts of Ḥimyar collapsed.[16]

Early Islam

The Aksumites' relations with the first Muslims are the subject of fascinating traditions and much historical speculation. As we have already seen, there was continuous interaction between the two sides of the Red Sea, even if we cannot always clearly define the precise political configurations.

One of the early converts to Islam and the first *mu'ezzin* (the person who sounds the call to prayer) was Bilal b. Ribah al Habashi, a freed slave of Ethiopian descent. Muslim traditions claim he was a particularly devout believer, having refused to renounce his new community even when placed in the hot sun with a huge boulder on his chest.

Around 615 CE, in the wake of their persecution in Mecca, the Prophet Muhammed sent a group of his followers, headed by Ǧa'far b. Abī Ṭālib and including one of his daughters, to seek asylum in Ethiopia with the Aksumite ruler, the *naǧāšī*. This event, remembered in Islam as the first *hiǧra* (migration, separation) has been the subject of numerous legends and much speculation.

The *naǧāšī* is said to have welcomed the refugees, in keeping with his kingdom's reputation for tolerance. Muslim tradition records that during their more than a decade's sojourn in Ethiopia these early Muslims converted several dozen locals to Islam, and that they later accompanied the migrants back to Arabia. Ethiopian Muslims (known as Ǧäbärti) point to this episode as the origin of their community. In later years this episode was cited as one of the reasons why Muhammed's armies did not conquer Ethiopia. The Prophet himself is claimed to have said, 'Leave the Ethiopians to themselves so long as they leave you alone' (*utrukfi al-habasha md tarakfikum*). It is also cited on both sides of contemporary debates as to whether it is proper for Muslims to migrate from majority non-Muslim countries.[17]

Given these early interactions between Aksumites and Muslims, it is not at all surprising that the text of the Quran contains several words which derive from Gəʿəz and appear in a religious context. For example, *ma'edah* in the Quran (Sura 5: Sura al ma'edah) is borrowed from the Gəʿəz *ma 'ədd*, meaning a table or banquet. Sura 5: verse 114, 'Jesus, son of Mary, prayed, "O Allah, our Lord! Send us from heaven *a table* spread with food as a feast for us!"' Some of these Ethiopic words – even when ultimately of Aramaic origin – came into Arabic and the Quran via direct and possibly oral transmission through Ethiopian merchants, mercenaries, slaves and perhaps even priests using the Gə'əz Scriptures.

Moreover, the conversion of a small number of Ethiopians to the new religion appears plausible. However, we must be more sceptical regarding the claim that among the early converts was the *nağāšī* himself. Although this pious claim is firmly embraced by many local Muslims, it is no less fiercely contested by others, including Christian Ethiopians and most non-Muslim scholars.

Until comparatively recently, Islam in Ethiopia and Eritrea has been a relatively neglected topic, especially when compared to the tremendous attention given to Christianity.[18] Only a handful

Tomb of the *Nağāšī*.

of studies have been devoted to exploring its history and development. More recently, however, new research and particularly archaeology have enabled scholars to fill in many of the gaps in our knowledge of Islam in the Horn.

Although it obviously arrived centuries after Christianity, from the ninth and tenth centuries onwards Islam entered Ethiopia via the northern coast, moving southward through Təgre into the highlands and the lake regions of the south. As was often the case in Africa, trade and trading networks played a crucial role in the diffusion of religion. As we have seen, trade also played an important role in the earliest spread of Christianity, but from the seventh century onwards this was no longer the case.

Of particular importance during this period was an archipelago of more than one hundred islands known as the Dahlak islands, which are in the Red Sea off the port of Massawa. They are set at the crossroads of trade, between not only Africa and Arabia but the Muslim world as a whole, stretching both into the Middle East and throughout the Indian Ocean. Although these islands occasionally came under the rule of the Ethiopian ruler, throughout most of their history they were under Muslim rule, either via Yemen or, from the late eleventh century, independently by a line of sultans. Funeral stelae found on the main island, Dahlak al-Kabīr, testify to the presence on the island of Muslims from Arabia, Syria, Iraq and Iran and even Georgia, Marrakesh and Valencia. Unfortunately, we know comparatively little about the network of Muslim traders who resided within Ethiopia during this period. The Dahlak islands declined from the twelfth century onwards. As we shall see in the next chapter, an alternative, more southerly, route for Islam into Ethiopia came into prominence during this period.

The decline of Aksum

The reign of Kaleb and his conquest of parts of the Arabian peninsula on behalf of the Christian world marked the apex of Aksumite power, prestige and particularly international fame. Many Ethiopian traditions view the period from the middle of

St Yared and Gäbrä Masqal, 20th century, mural.

the sixth century to the middle of the seventh century as a prosperous era that saw important developments in the evolution of both Church and state. Nevertheless, the first indications of the kingdom's decline began to appear.

Kaleb's purported heir Gäbrä Masqal ('the Servant/Slave of the Cross') is perhaps best remembered for his association with the development of Church music. According to tradition, St Yared, who in his early days was a poor student, was later gifted with extraordinary patience and persistence. He is credited with creating the entire corpus of Ethiopian Orthodox chants, *qene* (an important genre of improvised poetry and the notational system for the music). Some even credit him with not only Christian music, but music in general. Traditions claim he was transported to Paradise, where three angels in the guise of birds taught him music. According to another widespread tradition, Yared performed before King Gäbrä Masqal. The king accidentally speared the saint's foot, but both he and the saint were so entranced by the music that neither noticed.[19]

The complex circumstances behind the decline and fall of the Aksumite kingdom remain one of the great mysteries of its history.[20] Over time the population appears to have dispersed, with a particularly precipitous drop in population density in the Aksum area. With the spread of the population, political authority also appears to have become less centralized.[21]

A combination of ecological and political changes was behind the kingdom's deterioration. Certainly, the decline of trade, depletion of the land's resources and an extended period of climate change all successively weakened the kingdom. In the wake of these and coterminous changes in the international balance of power, political control waned and rebellions and upheavals ensued.

About a decade ago, the Ethiopian scholar Yohannes Gebre Selassie called attention to the possible impact of plague on the decline of Aksum.[22] The Justinian Plague, named for the Byzantine emperor, devastated large parts of the Mediterranean basin, the Near East and Europe from 541 to 549. It was the first known case of the widespread *Yersinia pestis* bacterium, which is borne by fleas on rats and causes bubonic plague. Although recent research has claimed that the mortality rates and social impact of this pandemic were not as serious as previously claimed, it was still clearly a watershed event in the ancient world. While the origins of the plague have not been determined and textual evidence for its presence in Aksum is lacking, many believe it spread from Central Asia. Some scholars suggest that it was brought to Aksum by soldiers returning from Ḥimyar. There is, moreover, also a strong case that it was spread to the Mediterranean via merchants from Aksum.

Yet another important factor in the decline of Aksum appears to have been the increased presence and aggressiveness of nomadic groups in northeast Africa. Though generally considered as a group of politically divided tribes sharing only language and a pastoralist economy, ancient Beğa society and its elites created complex political arrangements in their desert.[23] Emperor ʿEzana's inscriptions mention expeditions against the Beğa nomads during the period before his conversion to Christianity. During Kaleb's struggles with the Ḥimyarites, Emperor Justin I offered to send him additional troops. He urged Timothy III, the Coptic archbishop of Alexandria (517–35), to write on his behalf to Kaleb, promising logistical aid to the Aksumites from African troops, including the Blemmyes (Greek) (referred to as the Beğa in Arabic and Gəʿəz): 'For our part we will send, from Coptos, Berenike, and [the territory] of the men called Blemmyes and Nobades, a large army: our troops, by pushing through your lands, will reduce the entire country of the Ḥimyarite (i.e., Yūsuf ʾAsʾar Yathʾar), and he himself, to utter desolation and anathema.'[24]

In the last years of the sixth century the Sassanid Persians seriously challenged Ethiopian control of South Arabia, and by the turn of the century that region had been removed from the Aksumite sphere of influence. After 602 Aksum's access to export markets and freedom of navigation were considerably weakened. Although it was, in the past, often claimed that Adulis was burned down by an Arab expedition in circa 640, the evidence for this is equivocal. Coins have been found at the site from half a century later, but there is also evidence of a massive fire and widespread destruction. The consensus today is that the overflow of the Ḥaddas, a seasonal river, which was a vital water source for Adulis, led to the city's destruction in the late seventh or early eighth century.[25]

Danəʾel and Judith

Very little is known about northeast Africa from the seventh to tenth century. One of the more intriguing figures from this period is an official called *haṣani* Danəʾel, who is identified in three undated Gəʿəz inscriptions. The title *haṣani* literally means 'tutor' or 'guardian' and appears to have been used as a royal title until as late as the first quarter of the thirteenth century. It is related to the term for a very young (nursing) child (*haṣan*) and may later have been a source for one of the titles of the king, *aṣe*. According to his inscriptions Danəʾel, a court official, 'subjected the king of Aksum and made him cease ruling Aksum'.[26]

The tenth-century Arab author Ibn Hawqal reports that a queen 'killed the king who was known with the title of haṣani' and then ruled for about thirty years. Around the same time another anonymous Arab author told of a Yemeni who brought a zebra to Iraq 'from one of the regions of al-Habasha over which a woman reigns'.[27] Yet another tenth-century source quotes from a letter sent by an Ethiopian king to George III, a Nubian king who ruled in the last decades of the tenth century:

> The King of Abyssinia sent to the King of Nubia, a youth whose name was George, and made known to him how the Lord had chastened him, he and the inhabitants of his land. It was that a woman, a queen of Bani-Hamiway, had revolted against him and his country. She took captive many people and burned many cities, and destroyed churches and drove him (the king) from place to place . . . He the king said to him (George) in the letter which he sent to him: 'I desire that thou shouldst help me in the fatigue.'[28]

For many years scholars have sought to determine the identity of this queen and the region from which she came.[29] Legends developed that she was a Jewish queen, 'Gudit' or Yudit (Judith), Esato ('fire') or Esther. Moreover, many following in the footsteps of the Scottish explorer James Bruce, who visited Ethiopia from 1769 to 1772, claimed that she was a 'Falasha', identifying her with the so-called 'Black Jews of Ethiopia'. There are many reasons to reject this identification, including the fact that the ethnic term 'Falasha (Fälaśa)' does not appear to have been in use prior to the fifteenth or even sixteenth century, and that most of the existing narratives do not depict her as a member of this group, but rather as a Christian convert to Judaism.

The story of Judith exists in several versions. She is often said to have been a resident of Aksum, perhaps a member of the royal family reduced to prostitution. She was tricked by a local priest, who sought to have sexual relations with her and gifted her shoes made from the golden covering of the Ark of the Covenant. Mutilated and disgraced, she left Ethiopia. Eventually she met a Jewish ruler, whom she married and convinced to destroy Aksum in revenge for the indignity she had suffered. At this time the Ark of the Covenant was taken from Aksum and hidden.

By depicting her as a Jewess and her primary area of activity as Aksum, the Judith traditions mirror on numerous levels the major themes of the *Kəbrä Nägäśt*. This comparison is foreshadowed in some versions of her legend, which explicitly compare her beauty to that of Sheba. The relevant themes include a woman tricked into sexual relations with a man; revenge (symbolically by Mənilək, who betrays his father, and militarily by Judith, who conquers her tormentors); travel and return to Ethiopia, specifically Aksum; merchants as a source of information on a rival kingdom; and the Ark of the Covenant. Indeed, in both stories people of the priestly line trick people of royal blood through the Ark.

However, the contrasts between the two queens are no less indicative of the interrelatedness of the two stories. Sheba is, before meeting Solomon, a virgin. Judith makes her living as a prostitute. Sheba brings glory to Aksum. Judith brings destruction to Aksum. Sheba, through her son, brings the Ark; Judith leads to the Ark's departure. Sheba leaves Ethiopia and becomes an Israelite; Judith leaves and becomes a Jew. A royal woman is tricked into sexual relations with a king. A royal woman is tricked into sexual relations with a priest.

Despite the legendary character of her activities, it is not difficult to find 'remains' of Gudit's activity throughout the Aksum area. About 2 kilometres (1¼ mi.) west of the centre of Aksum is a collection of relatively small stelae in what is commonly referred to as the Gudit Stela Field.[30] In Təgray province near the town of 'Addi Akäwəh (Käwəh) there is a site called Mäqabər Gaʿəwa – literally 'the tomb of Gaʿəwa', yet another name for Gudit.[31] Although recent excavations indicate it is a Pre-Aksumite site, oral traditions strongly connect it to the rebel queen.

In fact, Gudit is only one of several women who is associated with (blamed for?) the decline of Aksum and the replacement of its ruling dynasty. According to one set of legends, a princess named

Statue of a woman in ʿAddi Akäwəh (Käwəh) associated with Judith.

Tərda' Gäbäz, the daughter of the last ruler of Aksum and a wife of a noble from Bugna, a region later associated with the Zagʷe dynasty, seized power to assure succession for her son and killed all but one of the members of the reigning dynasty.

According to other traditions, it was Mäsobä Wärq, the daughter of the Aksumite ruler Dəlna'od, who tricked her father into approving her marriage to a general from Bugna, Täklä Haymanot (not to be confused with the thirteenth-century monastic leader of this name), who eventually overthrew the Aksumites and established the Zagʷe in power.

We should be careful of giving too much credence to these stories. However, at least two points are of interest. First, all three (including the Gudit stories) suggest that a female member of the royal family of Aksum was responsible for their eventual overthrow. In addition, all three depict the 'new' dynasty as a group with familial links to the previous one. I return to this last point in the next chapter.

According to several medieval Arab authors, beginning in the ninth century the Ethiopian *nağāši* resided in a place called

Ku'bar/Ka'bar or Kafar/Kufar. The Baghdadi historian and geographer al-Ya'qūbi (d. 897) located this on the coast near the Dahlak islands. Somewhat later his compatriot al-Mas'ūdī (*c.* 886–956), sometimes known as the 'Herodotus of the Arabs', believed Ka'bar to be a huge city and the country's capital. Unfortunately, because these sources are vague regarding both the name and location of this site, we are unable to state anything about it with much certainty.[32]

Deaths on the Nile

Events in Ethiopia in the tenth and eleventh centuries cannot be fully appreciated unless we view them in the fuller context of the entire Nile basin. Between 950 and 1072 the Nile valley experienced a disastrous series of droughts. While the period from 300 to 900 experienced only eleven years of drought, in the century and a quarter from 950 to 1072 the number of dry periods totalled 26 years! More than half of the period from 1052 to 1072 was characterized by water scarcity and hence, in Egypt, disastrous food shortages. Indeed, not only was Egypt deprived of its traditional role as a food exporter, but it was unable to feed its own residents. Sources as varied as the medieval Muslim historians al-Maqrīzī (1364–1442) and Ibn Taghribirdi (1411–1470) as well as contemporary documents from the Cairo Genizah (a trove of Jewish documents saved because they contained the name of God) offer insight into the crises which ensued.[33] The seven years from 1065 to 1072 saw a famine of biblical proportion, which recalled the period of the Old Testament's Joseph. Although we lack documentation directly from Ethiopia, if the Nile failed to rise in Egypt throughout much of this period, drought probably prevailed in Ethiopia. Indeed, the Fatamid caliph is said to have believed that the Ethiopians had dammed the Nile and ordered the Coptic patriarch to intervene.[34]

It is important to put the decline of Aksum into the context of wider, more theoretical debates about the 'collapse' or 'resilience' of societies and civilizations. 'Rarely do societies collapse in an absolute and apocalyptic sense . . . Things can change profoundly, but fundamental elements of a society such as belief systems and ways of making a living retain their basic structure.'[35]

This certainly appears to have been true regarding Aksum and its kingdom. Although Aksum lost its place as the political centre of a powerful Christian monarchy, it continued to have rich religious, symbolic and historical significance. Indeed, many of the glorious traditions associated with Aksum appear to have arisen centuries after its political decline. However, there can be little doubt that over the centuries after 'Ezana and Kaleb, Christianity had become firmly entrenched, with both representatives among lay members and clergy spread throughout a wide area.

FIVE

A Legacy in Stone: The Zag^{W}e Dynasty

Saintly Usurpers? It becomes a little easier to reconstruct the history of Ethiopia, or at least its political configuration, in the twelfth century with the rise of a new dynastic line, known to historians as the Zag^{w}e. Nevertheless, the contemporary sources for the history of these monarchs are extremely limited.

Although we have hagiographies (*not* chronicles) for several of the Zag^{w}e kings, including Lalibäla, his wife Mäsqäl Kəbra, Yəmrəḥannä Krestos, Nä'akk^{w}eto Lä'ab and Ḥarbay, all of these were composed long after the reigns they commemorate.[1] Only the first of these has been adequately studied.[2] The life of Ḥarbay has not even been published. Ṭänṭäwədəm, who is one of the only Zag^{w}e rulers who left behind some contemporary records, including a land grant and a donation to a monastery, is apparently not commemorated by a *vita*. Or at least none has been found to date. The king lists which claim to record the successive Zag^{w}e rulers are inconsistent and vary from five to eleven names and cover a period of anywhere from 130 to 370 years.

The central paradox that historians have faced regarding the Zag^{w}e dynasty's leaders is that they are viewed simultaneously as illegitimate usurpers who replaced the Aksumite kings and saintly figures venerated by the Church. In fact, this contradiction can be resolved if we understand that the former image originated in the thirteenth and fourteenth centuries, when they represented a challenge to the newly reigning 'Solomonic' monarchs, while the latter exemplifies a later effort (mid-fifteenth century and beyond) to rehabilitate past rulers who were no longer a meaningful political threat.

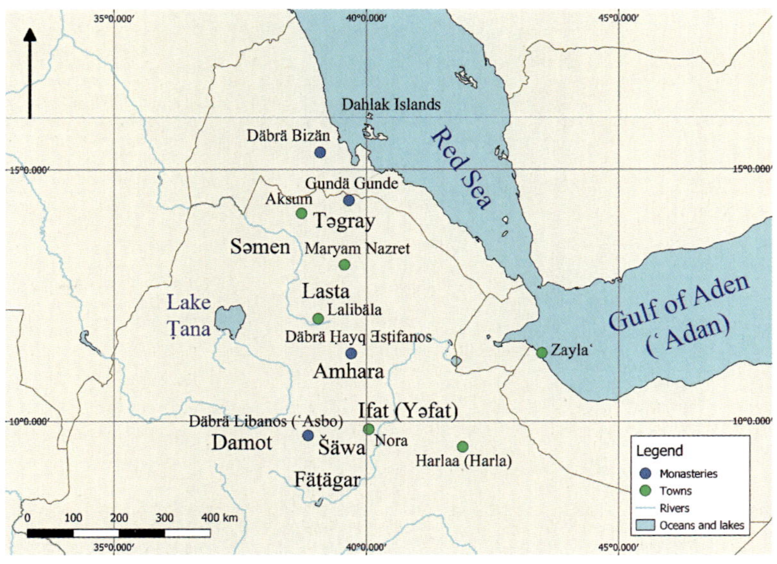

Medieval Ethiopia.

According to the received history, which was written long after their fall from power, the Zagʷe rose to power around the middle of the eleventh century. From their base in Lasta province they ruled Ethiopia for about a century and a half until 1270. Despite the attempts of some sources to link them to Queen Gudit and thus claim they were Jews, there appears to be little doubt that they were committed Christians, who both preserved and strengthened the religious traditions they inherited. As we shall discuss in a moment, the most visible expression of their religious devotion came in the form of rock-hewn and cave churches, particularly in the city that came to be known by the name of the dynasty's most famous ruler, Lalibäla.

According to this narrative, the Zagʷe were illegitimate kings because they were not Solomonic descendants of the earlier rulers of Aksum. They did not speak a Semitic language, but rather one of the many Agäw (Cushitic) dialects of the region. While according to later traditions they sought to bolster their claim to legitimacy by presenting themselves as 'Israelites', descendants of Moses and his wife Ṣiporah, they struggled to gain widespread recognition. Indeed, there also appear to have been traditions which linked them to Solomon through one of the Queen of Sheba's servant girls![3]

Yet, recently, historians have argued that there appears to be far more continuity between the Zag^{w}e and their Aksumite predecessors than we might expect if the former were sworn enemies and rivals of the latter. The archaeologist David Phillipson has long maintained that there are considerably stronger links between Zag^{w}e architecture and Aksumite (and even Pre-Aksumite) buildings than is generally credited.[4] Moreover, in a series of articles and

Zag^{w}e kings Lalibäla and Nä'akk^{w}eto Lä'ab in a 17th-century manuscript of the *Life of Yəmrəḥannä Krəstos*.

chapters, which have culminated in a groundbreaking book, the French scholar Marie-Laure Derat has offered a radically different understanding of the Zagʷe.[5] Noting that none of the contemporary sources refer to them by this name, she challenges much of the commonly accepted wisdom regarding this period and its dynasty. With a meticulous eye for nuance and detail she admirably fleshes out Taddesse Tamrat's suggestion that the rise of the new rulers shows not the 'signs of a sudden and dramatic advent to power of a new cadre of leadership . . . but only the culmination of a natural political development within the Christian kingdom'.[6]

The Zagʷe, or perhaps as they should be more appropriately designated based on their regional origin the Bugna/Bəgʷəna, Derat suggests, were not necessarily rivals of the Aksumites, nor did they present themselves as markedly different regarding language and style.[7] From their stronghold located in present-day Wällo, they proclaimed their claims to rule the kingdom. 'King Lalibala presented himself in the manner of an Aksumite king, thus seeking to emphasize his links to this ancient kingdom', including his use of the title *haṣani*.[8] King Ṭänṭäwədəm had the throne name Solomon.[9]

The Zagʷe, Derat suggests, were not (as is commonly claimed) originally from or limited to the Lasta region.[10] Lalibäla's wife Mäsqäl Kəbra appears to have had close ties to areas around the monastery of Däbrä Libanos of Šəmäzana, which is located near the modern border between Təgray and Eritrea.[11] (We should not forget that several of the traditions presented in the previous chapter claimed that there were kinship links between the last Aksumites and the first Zagʷe rulers.) Near the end of his reign King Lalibäla donated land to the monastery of lä-Mäṭaʿ zä'Abam, which is in modern Eritrea. King Ṭänṭäwədəm bestowed an engraved metal plate on an illuminated Gospel found at the monastery of Däbrä Libanos of Ham, also in Eritrea. The church of 'Ura Mäsqäl (Qirqos) holds a cross in honour of this king as well as land grants in his name.[12] Moreover, it has recently been suggested that important churches in Təgray, Gwaḥgot Iyäsus and Maryam Qiʿat, both near the town of 'Addigrat, and Maryam Qorqor in Gärʿalta, were constructed as part of an ambitious programme to assert Zagʷe authority over the local populations in that region.[13]

There is, moreover, 'no concrete evidence whatever that the Zagʷe spoke the Agäw language'.[14] Indeed, 'the Agäw identity of the dynasty is far from settled.'[15] Finally, Derat challenges the commonly accepted view that the Zagʷe were, in their own day, viewed as non-Solomonic usurpers, and in a dramatic reversal of conventional wisdom suggests that the later (post-1270) 'Solomonic' kings may have challenged the legitimacy of their predecessors to strengthen their own bona fides.[16]

The churches

Despite the lack of contemporary historical sources about the Zagʷe and the scarcity of literature from their period, the Zagʷe certainly left their mark on Ethiopia, especially in and around the city today named after their most famous ruler, Lalibäla. Originally known as Wärwär or Roḥa, it is believed to be named after the Syrian city of Edessa, which had been captured by Muslim armies in 1144. (This town was known as Othay-ar-Ruha in Arabic.)

According to its founding legend the plan for the city revealed to Lalibäla was a replica of Jerusalem. Toponymically, this is reflected in the presence of a stream called the Yordanos (Jordan), although that river does not, of course, flow through Jerusalem. To the northwest of the 'first' group of churches is an area called Awdä Fəṭḥ (Court of Judgment), which marks the place where Pontius Pilate condemned Jesus. Moreover, several buildings recall Aksumite churches, which themselves invoke sites in Jerusalem.

It must be noted that, although it is frequently referred to as the Zagʷe 'capital', the archaeological evidence does not clearly support the idea of a large urban settlement at the site. Neither can we definitively confirm that the Zagʷe made use of any permanent capital. On the other hand, evidence for a roving court, as was common in later periods, is similarly missing. What is certain is that Lalibäla contains a collection of buildings built over a period of many years, perhaps even centuries, which have in the course of time become important churches and sites of pilgrimage.

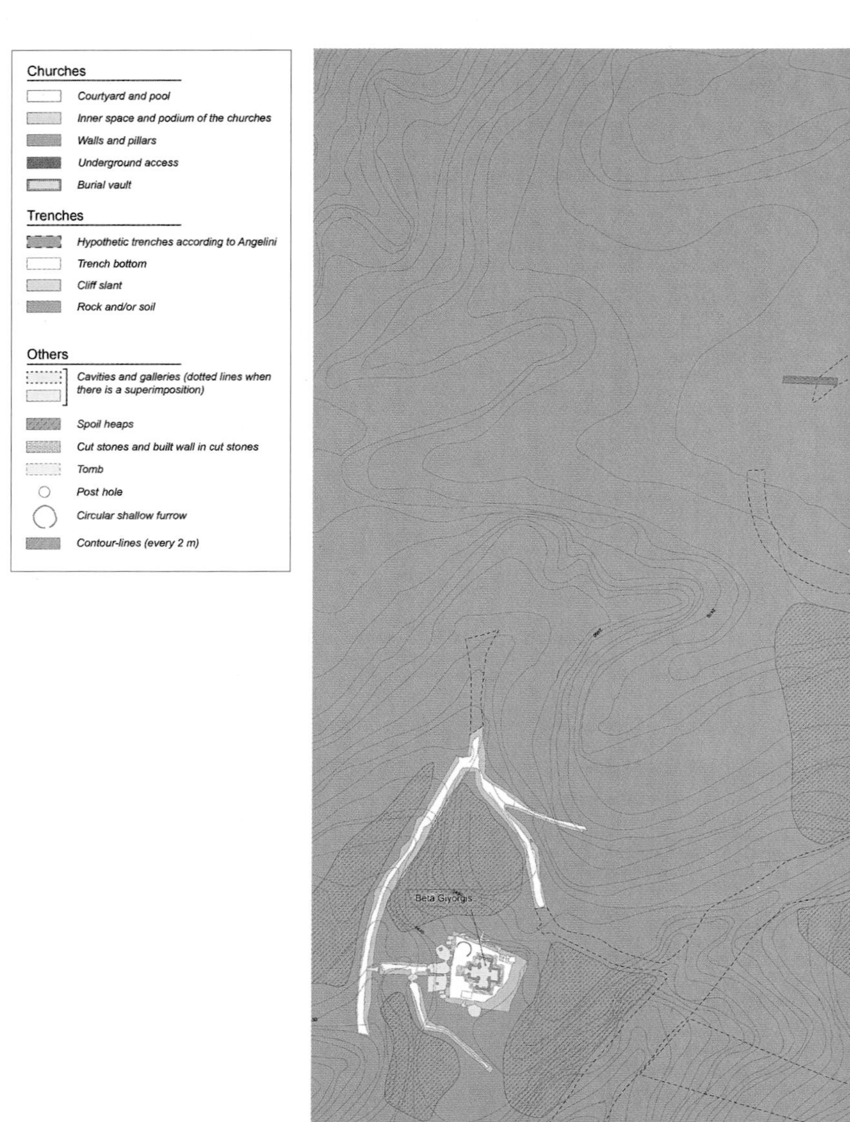
Churches
Courtyard and pool
Inner space and podium of the churches
Walls and pillars
Underground access
Burial vault
Trenches
Hypothetic trenches according to Angelini
Trench bottom
Cliff slant
Rock and/or soil
Others
Cavities and galleries (dotted lines when there is a superimposition)
Spoil heaps
Cut stones and built wall in cut stones
Tomb
Post hole
Circular shallow furrow
Contour-lines (every 2 m)
Beta Giyorgis
N

Betä Masqal
Betä Maryam
Betä Sellase
Betä Mädhane Aläm
Betä Dänagal
Jordan river
Betä Amanu'el
Betalehem
Betä Marqorewos
Dabra Libanos
Betä Gäbra'el Rufa'el

Lalibela.

The Christian highlands of Ethiopia are home to hundreds of rock-hewn churches. The tradition of such churches probably goes back to the Aksumite Period. Indeed, some scholars have speculated that this architectural phenomenon is a continuation of an earlier pre-Christian troglodyte tradition of cave shrines.[17] To be sure, at their simplest these shrines were established in pre-existing natural caves, but there were also many monumental structures fully or partially carved out of rock (frequently limestone and sandstone).

These churches, and particularly those of Lalibäla, are deserving of and have received full book-length treatments.[18] The limits of this volume make it possible only to scratch the surface of a subject which has both literal and figurative depth. The churches of Lalibäla are not a single group, they do not follow a single architectural plan, and perhaps most importantly they developed across time and express multiple meanings. There is ample evidence that several of the 'churches' were not originally constructed or excavated as religious shrines, but rather were fortresses or palaces which were later repurposed.[19] Once again, it must be stressed that, contrary to the view that the Zagʷe were rivals of the Aksumites, many of the buildings reveal affinities with Aksumite architecture, including the stelae. This is reflected not only in 'quoting' from specific Aksumite buildings, but in incorporating many earlier stylistic elements. All the churches reproduce the form of buildings constructed with facades, window frames and other standard features.

The northern complex of seven churches includes some of the most remarkable buildings. Mädḫane 'Aläm (the Saviour of the World, the Redeemer) is the largest of the churches (33.7 metres long, 23.7 metres wide and 11.5 metres high (110½ × 77¾ × 37¾ ft)) and is thought to be an architectural quotation of the metropolitan cathedral of Aksum Ṣəyon. According to the view that the Zagʷe were rivals of the Aksumite rulers, this church was intended to challenge and even supplant the great church of Aksum. We could just as easily suggest that the desire to construct a replica of Jerusalem/Aksum was a tribute to their predecessors as much as an act of defiance.[20]

Church of Mädhané Aläm/Mädḫane ʿAläm (the Saviour of the World, the Redeemer), Lalibäla.

Betä Maryam (the Church of Mary) was clearly hewn to serve as a church, although there may have been earlier excavations. It 'embraces a mélange of Eastern Christian influences [architecturally] which include Syriac as well as certain Coptic influence'.[21] In contrast to the lack of decoration in the Church of the Redeemer, which Jacques Mercier believes was built a few years later, it is richly ornamented, perhaps by Coptic artists.[22] It is the only church decorated with murals painted before the fall of the Zagʷe.[23] This includes Gospel scenes such as the Transfiguration and Annunciation, the miracle of the loaves and fish, Christ's meeting with the Samaritan lady and the flight of the Holy Family to Egypt, as well as portraits of saints. These appear to be related stylistically to the Church of Yəmrəḥannä Krestos.

Betä Dänagəl (the Church of the Virgin/Virgins), like the Church of the Redeemer, may have originally been a quotation of a church of the Virgins in Aksum, which itself echoes a nunnery in Jerusalem.[24] By the sixteenth century this interpretation had been superseded by an identification with the Virgin martyrs of Edessa, who died in the late fourteenth century.

Betä Qəddus Mika'el (Däbrä Sina) Mt Sinai and Betä Golgota (Golgotha) form a complex along with Betä Selassie, which Michael Gervers believes to be the last of the churches to be established; he dates them to the fifteenth century.[25] The first church references Mt Sinai, but since the introduction of a *tabot* dedicated to St Michael, the devotion to that saint/angel is its paramount focus. As the name of Betä Golgota indicates it is associated with the 'Hill of the Skull', which is identified in all four Gospels as the site of Christ's crucifixion. This is also, according to some traditions, the site of Adam's burial, where Christ's blood dripped down from the Cross and purified the first man from sin. From the middle of the fifteenth century onwards, however, this church came to be identified with the tomb of Lalibäla. At that time the emperor Zär'a Ya'qob donated a copy of *Gädlä Lalibäla* (Life of Lalibäla) to the church and a contemporary painter produced the first known image of the saint.

Betä Maryam (Church of Mary), Lalibäla.

Betä Amanu'el.

The second group of churches is found southeast of the first and includes four rock-hewn structures. Several of these can be clearly determined, based on their different styles and lack of conventional orientation, to have not been originally built as churches.

The church of Betä Amanu'el (St Emmanuel) is one of the four (along with Betä Maryam, Mädḫane 'Aläm and Betä Giyorgis (St George)) that are cut completely from the rock matrix (and the only such church in the eastern group). It closely simulates the visual effects of wood and stone found in such Aksumite churches as Däbrä Dammo. Indeed, Georg Gerster, in his important study *Churches in Rock*, suggested that 'if one did not have the monastery church of Dabra Dammo . . . one could nevertheless quite easily reconstruct the built-up original from the rock copy' due to the architect or builder's determination to be, if possible, more Aksumite than Aksum.[26]

Betä Giyorgis.

Finally, we turn to Betä Giyorgis, which stands to the west of the other two groups of churches. Its cruciform plan makes it the most visually arresting of all the Lalibäla churches. According to local tradition, when Lalibäla had completed the other churches, Giyorgis appeared to him, aggrieved that no church had been consecrated in his honour. The king immediately set out to rectify this omission.

Whatever the historical background to this church, Giyorgis is certainly among the most honoured of non-Ethiopian saints in the country. While veneration of him may date back to Aksumite times, his *vita* (or at least the current version) was translated from Arabic around the fifteenth century. He is depicted in art, both wall paintings and miniatures, even earlier. He is commemorated with both an annual and a monthly celebration. Indeed, the great Ethiopian victory over the Italians at Adwa in 1896 came on one of his monthly celebrations and Giyorgis is said to have appeared on the battlefield riding a white horse.

More traditionally, Giyorgis is remembered as an early convert (third or fourth century) to and martyr for Christianity. While various miracles are attributed to the saint and depicted in his iconography, from the fifteenth century onwards he is primarily depicted as an equestrian saint and credited with killing a dragon or serpent.

St George slaying the dragon and the Virgin Mary holding Christ, flanked by archangels, two panels from a double-sided pendant, Amhara or Tǝgrǝññya peoples, early 18th century, wood, tempera pigment and string.

According to church tradition, these churches, as well as the others in the Lalibäla complex, were all built during the reign of the king of the same name. While some scholars have loosely accepted this dating and contend that the buildings were built over a relatively short period, there is no compelling evidence that most of the churches were built in the thirteenth century.[27] Many scholars favour a more extended period of construction, and it must certainly be acknowledged that the buildings often reveal multiple excavations over a prolonged period. In the words of Derat,

> Evidence of several phases of excavation at the site affirms that the churches were not carved during a single program but, rather, were progressively rearranged and transformed. It is also known that entire sections of the site collapsed, but were cleared out, and were then recut, giving us the site as we see it today.[28]

Some argue that the earliest edifices, which were not originally intended as churches, might date from the seventh or eighth century, the end of the Aksumite Period, and that the Zag^{w}e Period witnessed the completion of a process.[29] Others put the creation of the last of these churches as late as the mid-fifteenth century and see it as part of a 'Solomonic' rehabilitation of the Zag^{w}e rulers after they no longer posed a threat.[30] Certainly the application of the name Lalibäla, as opposed to the earlier Roḥa-Wärwär, appears to originate from this later date, and the hagiographies of the Zag^{w}e rulers were composed in the fifteenth and sixteenth centuries and even later.

An Egyptian outpost

In the previous chapter, I quoted part of the king of Ethiopia's letter to the Nubian ruler George II, who ruled in the last decades of the tenth century. In this letter not only did the Ethiopian king complain of his dire political circumstances, but he expressed concern for the survival of the Church. In a letter partly quoted and partly summarized by the patriarch's biographer we read:

> for the sake of God and for the sake of the unity of the faith, and that thou shouldst write a letter on thy part to the father, the patriarch, in Misr, to beg him to absolve us and to absolve our lands and to pray for us, that God may remove from us and from our country this trial, and may grant to us that he (the patriarch) may consecrate for us a metropolitan, as was the custom of our fathers, and that he may pray for us, that God may remove His wrath from us. I have mentioned this to thee, O brother, for fear lest the Christian religion pass away and cease among us, for lo, six patriarchs have sat and have not paid attention to our lands, but they (the lands) are abandoned without a shepherd, and our bishops and our priests are dead, and the churches are ruined, and we have learned that this trial has come down upon us as a just judgement in return for what we did with the metropolitan.[31]

However dire the situation of the Church may have been in the last years of the tenth century, recent archaeological work clearly shows that by the middle of the eleventh century the connection between Egypt and Ethiopia not only had been restored but was flourishing.

In a recently published monograph Mikael Muehlbauer discusses three cruciform churches, Abrəha wä-Aṣbəḥa, Wəqro Ḉärqos and Mika'el Amba, all found in eastern Təgray. The author dates these churches to the mid-eleventh century and indicates that they may have links to the emergence of the the Zagʷe. If he is correct not only does this strengthen the case for the links to the Zagʷe to this northern province but this building programme also strengthens the claims for continuity between their architecture and that of late antiquity. The links with Fatimid Egypt are also impressive and significant.[32]

Another site in Təgray province that is particularly important in this respect is Maryam Nazret.[33] By combining numismatics, archaeology, oral traditions from locals and a few documents preserved in much later versions, scholars have recently offered a fascinating reconstruction of the area. The earliest building uncovered thus far at Nazret appears to be from the later part of the Aksumite Period.[34] Indeed, coins found at the site are from the seventh century and may be from the last Aksumite kings to mint coins.

Among the names associated with the location are 'Addi Abun ('the country [village] of the abun') or 'Addi Gebsi ('the country of the Egyptians'). The former refers to the presence of the graves of several Egyptian metropolitans at the site. In the middle of the twelfth century, the Egyptian Abuna Mika'el consecrated a Coptic church here. According to a dedicatory text which survives in a seventeenth- or eighteenth-century copy, Mika'el dedicated the church towards the end of his long reign as metropolitan of the Church in Ethiopia:

> And by the good pleasure of God I have ordained 27,000 priests and I have made monks [or nuns] 5,000 [persons] and I have baptized 50,000 persons in the rivers and in the churches and I beg God that he may have compassion on me and hide my sins in his mercy and I have built 70 churches.[35]

Site of Maryam Nazret, the episcopal seat in the 12th and 13th centuries.

In the same document he claims to have anointed seven kings and consecrated over 1,000 churches. Although the numbers cited are almost certainly exaggerated, Mika'el had served in Ethiopia for at least twenty years and possibly twice that time. Certainly, we know that only a few years before this the reigning king had written to the Coptic patriarch asking for a replacement for Mika'el, who was already quite elderly.

Clearly, Maryam Nazret was a major outpost of the Coptic Church in Ethiopia. Constructed according to architectural models found in Egyptian churches of the same period, it continued to be used for many centuries. It appears to have been the home base of an expatriate community – and Egyptian at that – with a nearby monastic satellite such as Golgota, whose presence and time frame require further enquiry. In the larger picture of things, we have clear evidence that by the middle of the twelfth century the connection with the Coptic Church had been restored and strengthened.[36]

Further evidence for a strong Coptic cultural presence is found in the wall paintings in the church dedicated to Yəmreḥannä Krəstos, who, as was noted above, was an important Zagʷe ruler. According to Ewa Balicka-Witakowska and Michael Gervers, the paintings in this church, which pre-date the buildings at Lalibäla, follow the eleventh- and twelfth-century Coptic artistic tradition. Indeed, they believe that they are 'not an offshoot of Coptic art, but the product of a genuine Coptic workshop'.[37] These paintings thus provide further evidence of major Coptic cultural impact in the Ethiopian highlands in the period of the Zagʷe.[38]

Monastic initiatives

In Chapter Four I discussed the rise of monasticism in the Aksumite Period. In the next chapter I shall have much more to say about the emergence of the militant monastic movements that clashed with the rulers of the thirteenth to fifteenth centuries. However, given the growth and spread of Christianity during the Post-Aksumite Period and the succeeding centuries as discussed above, monasticism and monasteries must have flourished and spread throughout the countryside. While over time many monasteries came to rely on the beneficence of kings and local rulers, who granted them land and donated religious items, they often began with an individual holy man establishing himself in an isolated location.

Among the best-remembered figures of the thirteenth century is Iyäsus Mo'a, who was born early in the century in Bägemder, southeast of Aksum and north of Lake Tana. In his thirties he went to the ancient site of Däbrä Dammo in the north and became a monk. He then travelled to Lake Ḥayq (in Amharic *ḥayq* means 'lake') and eventually established the monastery of Däbrä Ḥayq Ǝsṭifanos. Although it is claimed that the church there had already been established in Aksumite times, it was with his arrival that it came to prominence. Iyäsus Mo'a was appointed its first abbot circa 1248 by one of the last Zagʷe rulers, Nä'akkʷeto Lä'ab.

Despite his ties to this dynasty, Iyäsus Mo'a is said to have been instrumental in the rise of Yekunno Amlak and the 'Solomonic'

Lake Ḥayq, the site of Däbrä Ḥayq Ǝsṭifanos.

dynasty to power in the late thirteenth century. As a reward for this assistance, the new ruler granted a *kidan* (pact) which bestowed lands upon his monastery, expelled women and laypeople from the island, conceded it the right to offer asylum and gave 'one-third of the kingdom' to the Church. One of his disciples was named *'aqqabe säʿat* (lit. 'guardian of the hours'), a high-court official who was responsible for the ruler's schedule (a title previously held by the Təgrayan monastery of Däbrä Libanos of Šəmäzana). Over time, the monastery came to accumulate a vast collection of manuscripts. Among the important monks trained at this monastery were Täklä Haymanot, who was a direct student of Iyäsus Moʾa, and the important literary figure Giyorgis of Sägla (*c.* 1365–1425).

Before concluding my discussion of the vibrant Christian culture of this period, one further point must be raised. Alongside the riddle of the Zag^{w}e as usurper-saints is the remarkable fact that we do not possess any works of Ethiopic literature which can be firmly dated to their period. Is it possible that such devout Christian rulers did not have a single work composed or translated during a period of almost a century and a half? Can it possibly be that, during a period of land grants and a programme of church-building and with the active presence of Coptic artists, literature was somehow excluded from the realm of cultural creation? Perhaps this is the case, but at the very least manuscripts must have been copied. Yet only a single 'rather clumsily executed' illuminated manuscript survives from their period.[39] There may have been a deliberate suppression of any Zagwe Period compositions by their successors.[40] In any event, this is certainly a question which must be revisited.

Muslim settlements

As is usually the case, we know far less about the Muslim presence in medieval Ethiopia and Eritrea than about contemporary Christianity.[41] However, recent excavations have made it possible to expand our knowledge on the topic. In the previous chapter I noted the entry of Muslims and Islam to Ethiopia from the north via the Dahlak archipelago and the port of Massawa. The town of Bilet (today known as Kwiha) in Təgray offers a tantalizing glimpse into the composition of its Muslim population during the tenth to twelfth century. Of the forty or so funeral stelae found in the town, those which can be dated range from 361 AH (972 CE) to 554 AH (1159 CE). The use of Arabic in Kufic script, precise *hiğra* (Muslim calendric) dating, Quranic references and six-pointed Islamic stars (the Seal of Solomon) all indicate a significant degree of Islamization. Moreover, the *nisba* (lit. 'relations') which provide information on the genealogy of some of those buried at the site testify to their ties throughout the Muslim world.[42] Based on this evidence it would appear probable that the Muslim community of Ethiopia was far better established and had much stronger links to the wider Islamic world than has previously been suspected.[43]

Unfortunately, we lack any solid information regarding the relations between these Muslims (or others on the trade routes) and their Christian neighbours. In later periods we see Christian agriculturalists, Muslim merchants and pastoralists, and minorities of hunters, gatherers and craftsmen. However, we must be cautious about going beyond our sources and assuming that these religious-ethnic divisions of labour were already in place.

From the twelfth century onwards the Dahlak islands declined in importance and became more of a regional hub and less of a central focus of trade with the Islamic world.[44] At the same time, the port city of Zaylaʿ, located in present-day Somalia, rose in prominence and became the dominant entry point from the Gulf of Aden into the (southern) interior. Previously, this port had been a small local centre exporting products that could be obtained in and around the coastal region. It was neither deeply Islamized nor a gateway to inland trade routes. However, from the late twelfth century onwards it rose in importance. This southern route not only offered Muslim traders better access to the interior, but avoided the tax regime of the Rasūlid rulers of Yemen.[45] By the middle of the thirteenth century, it had become an important waystation for Middle Eastern and North African pilgrims bound for Mecca and Medina. Moreover, in addition to these transient visitors, scholars, merchants and slaves (both male and female) passed through Zaylaʿ. Indeed, during this period Ethiopian Muslims were sometimes referred to as Zaylaʿī.

Not surprisingly, this flourishing of trade led to the development of networks into the interior and the spread of Islam. Recent excavations in Harlaa (Hubat), which is located 120 kilometres (75 mi.) from the Red Sea between Dira Dawa (15 kilometres/9 mi.) and Harar (40 kilometres/25 mi.) at the midpoint between the highland and the lowland, have shed valuable light on these

Old view of Zaylaʿ, Somaliland, from *Le monde illustré* (12 February 1887).

Remains of a mosque in Harlaa.

processes. According to local legends, Harlaa was a 'city of giants' who were able to construct walls by lifting stones that no normal person could raise.[46] It was an entrepôt receiving and supplying goods and materials via both maritime and land-based trade networks over a large geographic area. Archaeological material attests to contacts – direct and indirect – with the Red Sea (shells), the western Indian Ocean (beads), China (ceramics), South and Central Asia, Egypt, the Ethiopian interior, the East African coast and the Persian/Arabian Gulf.

The population of Harlaa was a mixture of Muslims and non-Muslims, with both groups having local and foreign components. Three mosques have been identified in the town, as well as wells, fortification walls and at least three cemeteries. The non-locals included Arabs, Indians, Persians, Somalis and perhaps East Africans (Swahili). Muslim ritual slaughter pre-dated the construction of mosques, and the cemeteries suggest that, as is so often the case, Muslims arrived and Islamic institutions followed. A substantial proportion of the animals slaughtered for food were sheep and cattle, fish and fowl. The relative dearth of warthog and bushpig remains indicates that some residents observed Islamic dietary laws.[47] It must be stressed that Harlaa was not under the rule of the Zag^{w}e rulers.

Finally, it must be noted that preliminary excavations conducted in Harar, the most important Muslim town in the Horn of Africa, indicate that despite some traditions claiming an earlier foundation, it probably only emerged in the sixteenth century and may perhaps have had some links with the much earlier settlement at Harlaa.[48]

While merchants played a role in the spread of early Christianity in the Aksumite kingdom, the connection between trade and Islam was far more durable and enduring. Indeed, many would argue that trade and traders were the primary agents for the diffusion of the latter religion. Muslim traders who moved freely throughout the Christian kingdom during most periods often served as teachers as well. Formally educated religious teachers usually only arrived after the establishment of a Muslim community. Thus the spread of Muslims usually preceded the spread of Islam and conversion was often more common along trade routes and in commercial centres.

Great mosque of Nora.

Prayer room of the great mosque of Nora.

In this context it is useful to examine yet another Muslim site from this period, Nora, which is in Yəfat, northeastern Šawa. Thanks to the extensive work of a French team of researchers, we know more about this city than about almost any other location in this period. The main mosque dates from the fourteenth century. In all there are five mosques, which are architecturally dissimilar to those of the coast of the Red Sea and Indian Ocean. According to archaeologist Stéphane Pradines:

> The Nora mosques are stylistically linked to the settlements on the plains extending out towards Zayla' and Berbera [the coast around the area of modern Somalia]. This represents a simple indigenous architecture with almost no exogenous influence. The simplicity of the techniques used in the construction of these religious buildings is mainly due to the scarcity of readily-available materials and the fact they were difficult to use.

The style of mosque, says Pradines, 'could be called the "Adal" style or the mosques of Bilad al-Barbar'. Although it has been speculated that Nora's trade routes connected with the Dahlak islands,

Pradines claims that 'Nora depended mainly on contacts with Zayla' and Berbera and the settlements along the roads; the mosques of that area are all culturally and religiously interconnected.'[49]

The recent re-evaluation of the history of the Zag^{w}e marks a crucial pivot in the history of the Christian kingdom. Previous narratives described the period from the decline of Aksum to the rise of the 'Solomonic' rulers circa 1270 as a 'Dark Age' in which the ancient legacy of early Ethiopian civilization was interrupted by rivals and usurpers. Only with the restoration of the true heirs was the trajectory of history restored.

However, recent groundbreaking research has produced a paradigmatic shift. While the immediate Post-Aksumite Period remains disappointingly vague, the period of the Zag^{w}e can now be depicted as representing far more continuity than had previously been understood. Indeed, far from being a disruption it emerges as an important testimony to the legacy of Aksum. While the lack of contemporary literature remains both disappointing and intriguing, one cannot ignore the remarkable architectural and artistic achievements, which are by no means limited to the churches of Lalibäla. The geographic expanse and the strong ties to the Coptic Church are a testimony to the successes of these rulers.

Moreover, if this new understanding of the Zag^{w}e is accepted, the rise to power of a new dynasty in the late thirteenth century must also be revisited and reconfigured. Far from marking a 'restoration' of legitimate rulers who had been deposed by usurpers, it represents a remarkably successful attempt to lay claim to the identity and glory of past kings while discrediting their immediate predecessors. In the next chapter, I explore this new episode and its impact on Ethiopia's national legacy.

Excursus: the wanderings of Prester John

> I will fetch you a toothpicker now from the furthest inch of Asia, bring you the length of Prester John's foot, fetch you a hair off the great Cham's beard, do you any embassage to the Pygmies.
>
> WILLIAM SHAKESPEARE, *Much Ado about Nothing* (II.1)

Detail of Ethiopia and Prester John, enthroned, in a map of of the Indian Ocean by Diogo Homem, Queen Mary Atlas, *c.* 1559.

The period of the Zagwe was also the era in which the legend of a remarkable monarch began to circulate throughout Europe and the Middle East. Prester John (Latin: Pres[by]ter Iohannes) is the name of an imaginary Christian oriental priest king, lord of (one of) the three Indies. Like the Queen of Sheba, Prester John's fame seems to have grown in proportion to the lack of verifiable information about him. He was, like the Queen, linked to the Three Magi. While it was claimed that she was their ancestor, it was often claimed that he was their descendant.[50]

In other ways, Prester John might be compared to Emperor Haile Selassie I, particularly as Ras Tafari in the early twentieth century. If Prester John was a symbol of Christian power and pride beyond the borders of the Muslim world and a potential ally for Western Christians, Haile Selassie was an exemplar of Black power and independence beyond the grasp of the dominant White European world. While Haile Selassie differs, of course, in the fact that he was a real person and ruled Ethiopia, his role as the projection of foreign hopes and dreams in a time of distress does recall that of the Prester.

The Prester's land was said to be a place of wonder, containing unimaginable wealth as well as such sites as the Tower of Babel, Mount Olympus, the fountain of youth and the Ten Lost Tribes. He ruled over not only 72 kings, but a heterogeneous population which included dog-headed men, satyrs and giants. Yet none of this is of any value to the historian of Ethiopia or the 'Indies'. As Charles Fraser Beckingham, one of the greatest authorities on the Prester John legend, wrote, 'From the very first mention of Prester John most of what we are told about him could not possibly be true, and most of the little that could conceivably be true is inconsistent.'[51]

The earliest written reference to the king is found in the eight-volume *Chronica sive Historia de duabus civitatibus* (Chronicle or History of the Two Cities) authored by the German cleric Otto of Freising (Bavaria) in 1145, a year after the fall of Edessa, an event which spawned the Second Crusade. It appears probable that the legend had circulated orally for some time before this. John is said to have offered the major Western powers the possibility of an alliance to free the Holy Land from Muslim rule. Although the Prester was believed to live in 'India', as we have already seen this term was imprecise and could refer to a variety of locations. Over the course of time, Prester John appears to have 'migrated' from the Indian subcontinent to Mongol Central Asia, and in the time of the Portuguese exploration of Africa to Ethiopia. Of course, the fact that there was indeed a Christian kingdom in Ethiopia contributed to this idea. However, the more familiar foreigners became with the actual kingdom, the less reasonable the legendary aspects appeared.

Only comparatively recently have scholars given attention to the broader apocalyptic and eschatological background of the Prester John legend. According to a late seventh-century Syriac work known as *The Apocalypse of (Pseudo) Methodius*, the last Roman emperor, who would eventually destroy the Ishmaelites, would be an 'Ethiopian', a descendent of an Ethiopian princess named Kusheth or Kushyath, who had married the founder of Byzantion. Thus this Ethiopian ruler would fulfil the biblical prophecy 'Let Ethiopia hasten to stretch out its hand [surrender] to God' (Psalm 68:31b). This image of an Ethiopian saviour may very well be connected to Kaleb's mission to Nağrān, which we discussed in Chapter Four. Interestingly, this Apocalypse reveals close ties to the *Kəbrä Nägäśt* and would appear to be one of its sources, or perhaps the two share a common source.[52]

It must be stressed that however fascinating the stories of Prester John may be, they tell us nothing about Ethiopia itself. Like the legends and other depictions of the Queen of Sheba, they offer insight into the projections, hopes and fears of outside observers, rather than on-the-ground details about the African Christian kingdom of Ethiopia. Moreover, unlike the Sheba legends, in this case we cannot even claim that the aura of Prester John was adopted and adapted by Ethiopians. Neither Gə'əz nor Amharic are among the more than thirty languages in which the (fictional) letter from Prester John has appeared.

When the Franciscan Remedius Prutky visited Ethiopia in 1751–2 towards the end of the reign of Iyasu II (1730–55), he told the emperor that 'he was entitled [referred to] in Europe as Prester John and begged him to pronounce upon it.' Iyasu, however, was astonished to hear this and declared 'that the kings of Abyssinia had never been accustomed to call themselves by this name'. This is the first recorded pronouncement by an Ethiopian ruler on the name, although it seems probable that the Jesuits (among others) had used the term while in the country.

In a final historical reversal, in the sixteenth century not only was the Christian Kingdom of Ethiopia (of Prester John) unable to supply support for Europe in its battles against the Muslim world, but rather Europeans (Portuguese) had to come to the assistance of Ethiopia when the kingdom was threatened by powerful local Muslims and their allies.

SIX
A 'SOLOMONIC' 'RESTORATION'

During the twelfth and thirteenth centuries, the major coastal entry point into the Ethiopian highlands shifted from the Dahlak islands to the southern port of Zaylaʿ. This important change enabled Muslim traders to avoid a long passage through the areas ruled by the Zagʷe in favour of more hospitable Muslim-controlled regions. This move inevitably weakened these northern Christian rulers economically and benefited groups, both Christian and Muslim, living further south.

Around 1268 Yəkunno Amlak, a military political leader from Amhara, supported by local monastic allies, overthrew the last Zagʷe king, a son of Lalibäla, named Yətbaräk. Although the ascension to power of Yəkunno Amlak at the head of a new dynasty is often portrayed as a turning point in Ethiopian history, its immediate impact on the existing political realities should not be overestimated. The problems that he and his immediate successors confronted were not substantially different from those of previous rulers. By 1270 Yəkunno Amlak was able to suppress the remnants of Zagʷe resistance, but the nobility of Təgray do not appear to have been very impressed by this new upstart regime. It took decades until his heirs were able to effectively assert themselves in that northern region.

In 1285 Yəkunno Amlak was succeeded by his son Yagba Ṣəyon (r. 1285–94). But during the next five years chaos reigned and five of Yagba Ṣəyon's sons were elevated to and deposed from the throne. Only with the ascension of Wədəm Räʿad (r. 1299–1314) was a modicum of stability restored.

One important indication of the unusual circumstances which prevailed circa 1295 is a wooden altar tablet inscribed in Syriac by Athanasius, the Bishop of Ethiopia (Kuš), which has been photographed in a church near Asmara in present-day Eritrea. This object, 'which is the only ancient or medieval written object in Syriac script or language that has . . . been found in Ethiopia or Eritrea', appears to strengthen the claims that at the end of the thirteenth century a Syrian Orthodox metropolitan resided in the region.[1] We can only speculate as to whether this unusual arrangement was associated with the unsettled political situation.

This same period was also an important era for the political development of Islam in the region of Šäwa. Only a few years after the rise of Yəkunno Amlak to power, the Muslim Maḫzūmī dynasty which had controlled parts of eastern Šäwa was overthrown by a new dynasty known as the Walašma' after its founder Wālī'Asma'. This put an end to over half a century of decline and chaos among the Muslims of the area. The most vivid expression of this disarray was the frequent deposition and murder of rulers by rivals from within their own dynasty.

Wədəm Rä'ad was able to bequeath a relatively stable political situation to his son, 'Amdä Ṣəyon (r. 1314–44). With his ascension to power, Ethiopia entered an era of remarkable political stability. During a period of almost a century, from 1314 to 1412, only four emperors ruled the country.

During his reign, 'Amdä Ṣəyon confronted several issues that had immense strategic consequences for the entire region of the Horn. In 1316/17, shortly after he had assumed the throne, he undertook successful military campaigns against Goğğam to the northwest, Damot to the west and Hadiyya in the south – all of which were economically important. He then turned his attention to the rulers of several northern regions, who had continued to assert their independence.

In Endärta, southwestern Təgray, the regional governor, Ya'əbikä Əgzi', did not even mention 'Amdä Ṣəyon when he granted land to a local church in 1322. His impudence was rewarded by a brutal campaign in which 'Amdä Ṣəyon deposed him. 'Amdä Ṣəyon's campaign in Endärta was a crucial step in the consolidation of the new dynasty. Not only did it remove a significant political threat and place the northern areas under the firm control of the Amhara dynasty, it also enabled them to assert clearly and unequivocally their claim to be heirs of Solomon and Sheba. The *Kəbrä Nägäśt*, which I discussed in Chapter One, served as a charter legend for these 'Solomonic' rulers of Ethiopia. However, it must be noted that the work appears to have emerged (re-emerged?) not in the court of 'Amdä Ṣəyon or among his monastic allies, but rather under the auspices of a rival ruler in the province of Təgray.[2] Thus a document intended to assert the primacy of the Təgrayan nobility came to serve a new southern ruling group for the next 650 years.

The successful adoption of a Solomonic–Aksumite pedigree was not the only case of 'identity theft' that marked the early fourteenth century. As I noted in the Prologue to this volume, throughout much of history the designation 'Ethiopians' or 'Ethiopia' was primarily used to refer to the Sudanese kingdom of Nubia. In this context, it is therefore revealing to note that the term appears no less than 122 times in the *Kəbrä Nägäśt*.[3]

Indeed, it has recently been claimed that in the late thirteenth and early fourteenth centuries the 'Solomonic' kings sought to supersede the fading Nubian rulers and began to position themselves as the true 'Ethiopians' and protectors of Eastern Christianity. One of the most interesting consequences of this exchange was the appropriation of the story of Queen Candace in Acts 8:27–39. Indeed, when the Portuguese Jesuit Francisco Álvares visited Ethiopia in the 1520s, he was explicitly told that Queen Candace resided in Aksum.[4]

The glorious victories

'Amdä Ṣəyon is generally considered one of the most important rulers of medieval Ethiopia. While this evaluation has much merit, we must be cautious not to read the comparative wealth of sources on his reign as an indication of his achievements. Beginning in 1332 he carried out a series of campaigns against several local Muslim sultanates. These battles and his triumphs are recounted and celebrated in what is one of the most widely published and studied texts in Gəʿəz literature.[5] Scholars have used it not only to reconstruct his military campaign, but to garner valuable insights on the character of his army and the political organization of the fourteenth century.

However, there is to this day no scholarly consensus as to when this text was composed. While some scholars believe it to be a contemporaneous account of the events it narrates, others date it more than a century later and contend that it reflects the realities of that later period. Most recently Bertrand Hirsch has challenged its historical value and characterized it as a work of 'fiction épique'. He believes that much of its narrative is based not on events of the mid-fourteenth century but on battles that took place at least a century later.[6] Obviously, we must be cautious regarding a far-reaching reconstruction that relies solely or largely on this one controversial central text.

In 1332 the ruler of Hadiyya, Amano, refused to pay tribute to the emperor. When he was defeated, he fled to Ifat. The leader of Ifat, Ṣabr al-dīn, who had previously been an ally of the Christian ruler, then staged a more general rebellion seeking to depose the 'King of Zion'. ʿAmdä Ṣəyon had to send troops to various regions, including Səmen, Wägara and Ṣallamt. He deposed the rebel ruler and appointed another member of the ruling family as his representative. He then turned his attention to ʿAdal, where he achieved another stunning victory.

Thus the sultan of Ifat became a satrap of the Christian king. Indeed, Al-'Umarī, a Damascus-born author writing from Egypt circa 1340, recounts that the seven Muslim kingdoms of 'the country of Zayla" were independent of each other but paid tribute to the Christian king, who controlled their political fates.[7]

It is important to stress that the ability of ʿAmdä Ṣəyon and his successors to impose themselves on different districts of the country varied sharply from area to area and from period to period. There were, of course, core areas of the kingdom in which the emperor sought to directly exercise his power. In others, he appointed loyalists who had demonstrated their fealty through their service in battle or at the court. In still other provinces, the king had to be satisfied with 'indirect rule' in which he chose a member of the local ruling family to be his representative. Finally, there were ambiguous cases in which regional nobles whom the king viewed as vassals considered themselves to be allies; the 'tribute' they sent to the emperor was, by their way of thinking, a 'gift' made on a voluntary basis. The locals were almost always seeking to assert their autonomy, while the kings were inevitably seeking stronger and more direct control.

Perhaps the most vivid expression of this power dynamic was the royal court (*kätäma*), a tent city which moved from place to place in keeping with the political and military needs of the ruler. Because of an 'out of sight, out of mind' mentality, kings often had to appear in troubled areas and assert their supremacy. Once they arrived, they imposed themselves on the locals, 'eating' their resources and reminding recalcitrant residents of their obligations. In the most central areas (the term 'central' here defines a type of rule rather than a specific physical location) the king's presence was more onerous than an honour and left the residents impoverished.

While the wars with the various Muslim sultanates were designed to give the Christian kings control over the crucial trade routes to the coast, a much broader theme was the ownership of land.[8] In Chapter Two I briefly set out some of the details of Ethiopia and Eritrea's long history of agriculture. It is worthwhile to offer more of an overview here. Throughout the northern Horn a variety of grains and legumes were cultivated. At different elevations mountainous regions were home to different crops.[9]

In theory, at least, all land in the country belonged to God and through Him to the reigning monarch. Typically, the ruler granted land – or more accurately the rights to collect taxes or tribute from the peasants living on the property – to 'nobles', loyal servants or churches. These grants of *g*ʷ*elt* land were inherently unstable as the king could expand or reduce an individual's or institution's holdings at any time. In contrast, many local farmers possessed inheritable rights to land referred to as *rəst*, which were relatively stable. Thus while it is common to refer to Ethiopian land tenure as a form of feudalism, it differed from the European model in several respects.[10]

Since often only Christians had *rəst* rights, non-Christians were forced to work on rented land or supplement their income in other ways. In many cases these groups were socially despised craftworkers and hunters. Perhaps the most discussed in recent years of the former were the Betä Ǝsraʾel, 'Fälaša' (Falasha), who were potters, weavers and smiths.[11] Significantly, the term *fälasawi* by which they were pejoratively identified can mean 'landless', 'wanderer' and 'monk'.

Far more numerous were the resident Muslims, who, as we have seen, were often pastoralists and merchants and hence had a very different relationship with land. Like other non-Christians they were generally denied ownership of land. Indeed, a proverb stated: 'Heaven has no pillars, the Muslim has no *rəst*.'

Finally, it must be noted that the poor in medieval Ethiopia were numerous and very visible. Most of these were the elderly, the young, and others who were unable to work. To a considerable degree these survived thanks to religious charity, whether Christian alms or Muslim *zaqat*. Indeed, Ethiopia was unusual in sub-Saharan Africa in possessing a clear system of merit acquired through charity.[12] Both Muslims and Christians believed that assisting the poor was of spiritual benefit to the donor, and not just material benefit to the recipient. Moreover, this leads directly to my next topic: there were ideologies surrounding voluntary poverty in the form of asceticism and chastity. To a considerable degree the religious landscape of Christian Ethiopia was dominated by figures who deliberately forsook the trappings of wealth and worldly success to live lives of abnegation and renunciation in the country's growing number of monastic communities.

Monastic movements

In the realm of Church life, the most important theme of the fourteenth and fifteenth centuries was the emergence of militant monastic movements which clashed with successive emperors and strongly represented local (versus national) interests.

Each of these monastic movements represented an attempt by regional groups to oppose the encroachment of the Solomonic kings on traditional autonomy and privileges. As the kings expanded their domain and reduced regional rulers to vassal status, some members of these ruling families abandoned the realm of overt politics and took up a monastic life. Although Ethiopian monasteries had probably always served as refuges or prisons for political failures, malcontents and those seeking respite from the outside world, the changing political circumstances of the fourteenth and fifteenth centuries dramatically increased the incidence of this phenomenon as local rulers fell under the control of the Solomonic kings.[13]

It was Šäwa province which first came under Solomonic domination, and it was here too that we witness the earliest development of a new militant monastic movement. The flowering of monasticism in this southern province is noteworthy because monasticism, like Christianity itself, appears to have only been established in this region in the second half of the thirteenth century under the auspices of St Täklä Haymanot. Born in Šäwa in the first half of the thirteenth century, he was educated by his father, who was a priest, and then studied with the famous holy man Bäṣälota Mika'el (and perhaps also with Iyäsus Mo'a), before returning home and founding the monastery of Däbrä Asbo. He is said to have been an active missionary. At the end of his life, he secluded himself in a cave and stood for so long that one of his legs broke off – he is almost always depicted in this pose.

In the fourteenth century his monastic descendants, led by the Abbot of Däbrä Asbo (later renamed Däbrä Libanos) and the anchorite Bäṣälota Mika'el, challenged the emperor 'Amdä Ṣəyon and his son Säyfä Arʿad over their marital practices and interventions in ecclesiastical matters. They were tortured and violently punished.[14]

The second of these monastic movements, which was named after its founder, the fourteenth-century monk Abba Ewosṭatewos, flourished in the northern province of Təgray and in Eritrea. Around 1300 the saint established the monastery of Däbrä Ṣärabi in the former. Eventually, however, its spiritual centre was in the Eritrean monastery of Däbrä Bizan, which developed into one of the Church's wealthiest religious centres. The Ewosṭatian

Täklä Haymanot, from an illuminated manuscript, 18th century.

movement championed such religious practices as the Saturday Sabbath in opposition to the Egyptian metropolitans and the dictates of the Solomonic rulers. Eventually Ewosṭatewos and some of his followers chose exile and are said to have settled in Armenia. However, they did not totally abandon their fight and in the fifteenth century their position became the official position of the Church.[15]

Perhaps the most curious movement of this period arose among the Betä Ǝsraʾel. Once again, the emergence of militant monks and in this case perhaps the ethnic group itself is linked to their opposition to the Solomonic kings. Although initially identified as inchoate groups of *ayhud*, literally Jews (rebels), over the

Abuna Ewosṭatewos, from an illuminated manuscript of *Täʾammerä Maryam* (Miracles of Mary), 16th–17th century.

course of the fourteenth and fifteenth centuries this group came to be identified by its distinctive non-Christian religious identity. The specific term used by outsiders, *Fälaśa*, does not appear to have been used for this community before the fifteenth and perhaps the sixteenth century. Ethiopian Christian monks are said to have joined the group and played a vital role in translating Scripture, composing texts and defining the Betä Ǝsraʾel's identity. Thus, to this day, many features of their 'Jewish' practice can be shown to have clear parallels with the hierarchy, sacred texts, liturgy and religious vocabulary of the Ethiopian Orthodox Church.[16]

Finally, there are the Stephanites or Ǝsṭifanosites, named after their founder, Abba Ǝsṭifanos. Since this group came to prominence in the middle of the fifteenth century, in opposition to the powerful ruler Zär'a Ya'qob's attempts to promulgate the cult of Mary and the Cross, I shall have cause to discuss them again in the next chapter.[17]

Our ability to reconstruct the history of these movements and the lives of individual holy men owes much to the existence of a vast corpus of hagiographic texts which recount their achievements in great detail and with great enthusiasm. Although many of these hagiographies were written long after the deaths of the saints they commemorate, when carefully read they provide much useful information regarding these heroes of the Church and their times.

Hagiographic literature is, of course, not confined to the Ethiopian Church. Beginning in the Aksumite Period, lives of saints and martyrs were translated from Greek. In later periods Arabic was the primary *Vorlage*. (While many of these clearly arrived in Ethiopia via its link with the Coptic Church, there are also works which, while clearly translated from Arabic, appear 'to be connected to the cultural milieu on the opposite shore of the Red Sea, in the area between the Sinai Peninsula and South Arabia'.[18])

In the fourteenth century, Gəʿəz literature takes an important step with the composition of original works concerned with holy men, including monks and kings, who were either locally born

Prayer house in a Betä Ǝsraʾel village, 1970s.

or carried out their most important activities in Ethiopia. A few works commemorating the early Ethiopian and Eritrean saints of the period after 'Ezana's conversion may have been the first of these to be composed. In the coming centuries this literature would grow to include over two hundred accounts, often composed at the home monastery of the saint. In this context, it is also interesting to note that in addition to their ritual differences and political stance, the different monastic movements also developed their own artistic traditions.[19]

Conversions

The expansion of the control of the Christian kingdom under 'Amdä Ṣəyon and his successors gave them dominance over a vast area, which was still inhabited by Muslims and a multitude of groups following local religions. This is, of course, not to say that, even in the most ancient parts of the kingdom, all, or perhaps even most, residents were Christian believers. Certainly, there were many ethnic groups, particularly those associated with crafts (smiths, weavers, potters), targeted with opprobrium and whose professions were 'despised' and thus avoided by Christians.

Moreover, the de facto and *de jure* leaders of Christianity were at best ambivalent about the spread of Christianity. The Egyptian abun was sensitive to the plight of his co-religionists in Egypt. Although the fourteenth-century metropolitan Ya'qob is remembered for organizing his allies to missionize, he was an exception.[20] Successive rulers not only valued the services provided by Muslim merchants but were aware that the Church frowned upon trafficking Christians as slaves. Thus at times their economic interests conflicted with the intentions of the Church. Moreover, there is little reason to believe that in this period (or even later) Ethiopian Christians viewed Christianity as a universal faith which welcomed all individuals regardless of ethnicity and social position.

It must be stressed that, unlike most modern Christian missionaries, the holy men who spread the Orthodox faith believed in the power of their opponents. Their success was derived from the greater strength of their God, who was often portrayed as defeating the representatives of these lesser spiritual beings in combat. It should also be noted that, although these battles took place in the context of an expanding Christian kingdom, for much of the thirteenth and fourteenth centuries many of these monastic missionaries were not direct representatives of the state's power. Some (like Iyäsus Mo'a and Täklä Haymanot) were active far beyond the effective borders of the kingdom; others, like the 'rebel' monks of Däbrä Libanos (Asbo), fled or were sent into non-Christian areas beyond the Awash river or around Lake Zway by rulers who viewed this exile as a way to detach them from their power base of believers. Thus conversion to Christianity was not necessarily viewed as political submission.[21]

Finally, these conversions are usually not depicted as long, drawn-out processes. Frequently it appears that the holy man moved on quickly after his success, leaving converts with limited knowledge of their new faith, living their daily lives in much the same manner as they had previously and with very limited access, if any, to holy books or clergy. In fact, it is sometimes startling to see how quickly converts moved from conversion to roles of Christian religious leadership. Given the nature of our sources, it is usually impossible to make any claims about the 'authenticity' of such conversions. In most cases many local religious elements were retained and, along the way, Christianity was itself transformed.

It is, of course, difficult to reconstruct the practices and belief systems of many of these groups since they left no written records. Obviously, the depictions of these peoples in Christian texts must be treated with caution since they are the creations of (generally hostile) outsiders. Moreover, since many of these sources are hagiographic, we must always be on the lookout for standardization of narratives and the importation of biblical tropes.

As we have already seen in the case of Däbrä Dammo and the images found in modern depictions of the Solomon and Sheba story, Christians are often said to have claimed control of a holy space by defeating a serpent/dragon (*arwe*) who was venerated by the local people. Of course, this theme is by no means limited to Ethiopia and is found in such widespread traditions as that of St Patrick, who drove the snakes out of Ireland, and

St George (Giyorgis), who as we mentioned earlier was greatly venerated in Ethiopia.[22]

If serpents were one expression of the demonic forces challenging Christianity, their personification took form through a variety of local cult leaders almost inevitably described in pejorative terms. These were often associated in the eyes of their Christian opponents not with gods or even lesser divinities but with demons.

Recently, however, some archaeological work has been done to fill in the gaps, especially regarding funerary practices.[23] In Chapter Two, I discussed the construction and significance of Aksumite stelae. Recently, several scholars have highlighted the widespread phenomenon of megalithic monuments as funeral markers throughout a broad geographical area of central Ethiopia. Although much greater in number than the Aksumite, they are far smaller.[24] Yet another form of funerary architecture is the tumulus, a man-made mound of stones and/or other material covering a grave site.

One such traditional culture was first described in detail by François-Xavier Fauvelle and Bertrand Poissonnier less than a decade ago.[25] Designated as the 'Šay' (Shay) culture after the name of a nearby river, it is once again best known to us through funeral tumuli. Often these tumuli are family tombs containing several generations, which departs from the standard Christian or Muslim practice. Although there are many aspects of this 'pagan' culture which remain to be elucidated, it is already possible to reconstruct some interesting cultural dynamics.

The Šay existed from the tenth century to the fourteenth. While it seems likely that many locals had converted to Christianity by the fourteenth century, it would be a stretch to describe the Šay as a stronghold of Ethiopian Christianity. Some of the evidence indicates a complex religious situation not unlike that which existed in the Aksum region a thousand years earlier. Materials that resemble Christian crosses and symbols which appear to be based on Ethiopic script are found alongside decidedly non-Christian elements. 'However local-religious these funerary practices remained, they displayed a discreet Christian veneer, or alternatively, that however fully Christian the beliefs of the people

Selection of ornaments of Šay culture, Tätär Gur.

were, their funerary practices retained a strongly local tinge.'[26] This is in keeping with the more general phenomenon of 'adhesion', which used to describe the addition of a new religion (in this case Christianity) to existing beliefs and practices rather than a dramatic break from one to another.[27]

In addition, these burial sites contain a wealth of luxury bracelets, necklaces and clothing. Most notable are the glass beads that originated in Egypt, Sri Lanka, Indonesia and China. Indeed, in some cases these appear in greater numbers than in comparable Muslim sites, although this may be the result of better preservation.

The Šay culture and other similar sites caution us not to dismiss the local religious environment as merely pre-Christian or pre-Muslim, but to attempt to engage them as comprehensive religious systems which we still struggle to properly reconstruct.

In the century or so after the rise to power of the Amhara dynasty the Christian kingdom greatly expanded and spread its political influence throughout the highlands. However, many aspects of its tenure and control remained fragile. The neighbouring Muslim sultanates were resistant to Christian domination. Much of the population had adopted Christianity only superficially, if at all. Moreover, conflicts with the emerging monastic movements meant that even the most elite corps of Christians were not necessarily loyal subjects of the realm.

About a century after the rise to power of the new dynasty, dramatic changes took place both within Christian life and within the kingdom itself. While these did not completely resolve the challenges of the Ethiopian state, they presented a template that would shape not only its future, but much of the understanding of its past.

SEVEN
In the Name of the Father and the Son

The period from 1380 to 1478 represents a cultural watershed in Ethiopian Christian history. Remarkable changes took place in the life of the Church and its role in the lives of the local population. Indeed, while by no means denying the antiquity of Christianity in Ethiopia and Eritrea, it is only a slight exaggeration to say that the late fourteenth century and first half of the fifteenth century was a formative period in Ethiopian Church history. Many of the most important and recognizable features of the Church can be dated to this era.

One of the primary purposes of this chapter is to examine how Christianity became embedded in the lives of believers. Thus while certainly not ignoring the importance of literature, much of my emphasis will be on the visual, emotional, calendric and bodily aspects of Christian observance.[1]

One of the challenges of presenting this material clearly is that the various uses of symbols were multi-levelled and interwoven. While it is convenient and perhaps necessary to divide these religious features into artistic, literary, ritual and political elements, such division inevitably separates phenomena that were intimately linked. For example, the promulgation of the cult of the Blessed Virgin Mary included the introduction of annual and monthly celebrations, the translation and composition of literary and liturgical works, and the creation of various forms of visual art, including icons and manuscript illuminations. Similarly, the dissemination of the veneration of the Cross involved calendric innovations, literary expressions, physical representations and even the embodiment of this symbol on the flesh of believers. Moreover, in both cases we cannot ignore the instrumental power of these symbols. For the medieval Ethiopian believer, Mary and the Cross were not only dominant images but potent forces capable of changing people's lives.

In her recent study of musicians in the modern Ethiopian diaspora ethnomusicologist Kay Kaufman Shelemay has explored the 'intensely multisensory [experience of] Ethiopian Christian liturgical performance'. While most of her evidence is drawn from late twentieth- and early twenty-first-century observations, she aptly shows that already in the mid-sixteenth century Portuguese Jesuits noted the 'heightened emotional impact of both participants and listeners'.[2]

Throughout this volume I have referred to different works of literature. Later in this chapter I expand upon this to offer a more general survey of Christian writings. However, I must stress that it is my deepest intention to avoid a litero-centric approach. On the one hand, literary works, along with architectural and artistic sources, are often our only basis for the reconstruction of ancient and medieval culture. On the other, it would be a grave mistake to assume that believers' primary experience of their faith was mediated through literature.

The Christianization of time

The constant interplay of feasts and fasts is one of the most obvious features of the Christian liturgical year. According to most reckonings, Ethiopian Christian clergy observe over 250 fast days a year, while members of the laity abstain on 'only' 180 days.[3] While some of these observances are marked by total abstinence from food or drink, most involve a vegan diet excluding all animal-based foods (eggs, meat, dairy), with a single restricted meal late in the day. Among the lengthiest and most important periods of fast were Lent (*'Abiy ṣom*), which extends for 56 days, Advent (*Ṣoma ledat*) for forty days, and the fast of the Apostles (*Ṣoma hawaryat*), which begins after Pentecost. Many devotees also fast every Wednesday and Friday.

The disciples of Abba Ewosṭatewos emerged in Təgray and Eritrea and strongly supported the observance of a Saturday Sabbath. By the last quarter of the fourteenth century, they were on the verge of becoming a separatist church as they no longer accepted the consecration of priests by the Egyptian metropolitan. Thus a limited corps of previously consecrated clergy was their only tenuous link to the rest of the Church. The self-imposed exile of Ewosṭatewos and some of his disciples to Armenia was probably motivated at least in part by their search for an alternative source of legitimation.

Emperor Dawit (r. 1382–1413) was favourably inclined to the Ewosṭatians and ceased their persecution. Although he may have intended to merely tolerate their position on the Sabbaths, his decision was a major victory for these dissidents. However, his second son, Yəṣḥaq (r. 1414–29/30), who inherited the throne after the brief reign of his brother Tewodros, was not generally tolerant on religious matters, reversed this position and sought to reconcile them by force.

One of the characteristics of the medieval rebel monastic movements was their refusal to accept royal donations of land and other forms of patronage. In Ethiopia, as in much of the world, the exchange of gifts represented much more than mere financial and material transactions. Thus the refusal to accept royal beneficence was not just part of an ascetic ethos, but a declaration of independence and autonomy.[4]

As Donald Crummey, the foremost authority on land policy in Solomonic Ethiopia, noted, 'Emperor Dawit, who reigned from 1380 to 1412, was a key transitional figure from the confrontations of the fourteenth century to a new synthesis and integration which marked church–state relations in the fifteenth century.'[5] Under his leadership, several monasteries that had previously rejected royal grants began to accept such donations.

While there is no disputing the claim that much of this activity was intended to strengthen Church–state relations and garner support from the clergy, we should not ignore the effect that such a policy had on the Ethiopian landscape. Accordingly, churches and monasteries were among the few massive structures found in the Ethiopian countryside. Their presence must inevitably have been understood as a testimony to the power of the faith they housed and represented. As Marie-Laure Derat has argued with characteristic perspicuity, they marked yet another expression of royal power.[6]

Zär'a Ya'qob, who was the youngest son of Dawit and reigned from 1434 to 1468, however, moved to confirm the Ewosṭatian position as the official position of the Church. In 1442, when the *de jure* leaders of the Church, the Egyptian metropolitans Mika'el and Gabrəʾel, were still supporting the Alexandrian practice, Zär'a Ya'qob wrote to the Ethiopian community in Jerusalem as follows: 'I hereby send you this book of *Senodos*, so that you can get consolation from it on the days of the First Sabbaths and Sundays.'[7]

Among the many churches Zär'a Ya'qob is credited with building, special mention should be made of the church of Däbrä Məṭmaq (Monastery of the Baptistry), which he had constructed in 1441. The church was built following the destruction of a similarly named Monastery of the Baptistry (al-Maǧtas) in Egypt in 1437/8. Only in 1441 did news of its destruction reach Ethiopia. Almost immediately, Emperor Zär'a Ya'qob ordered a replacement to be constructed in the heart of his kingdom. It is significant that Zär'a Ya'qob chose *this* church as the site for a crucial council in 1449 at which he resolved the controversy over the observance of the Saturday Sabbath. Where better to assert his authority over the Church than at a site that was itself a visible testimony to his orthodoxy, devotion and power?

While his decision was certainly motivated by shrewd political considerations, the confirmation of the two Sabbaths was in keeping with his overall policy of embedding as many Christian observances as possible in the daily routine of Christian life. Moreover, it offers a striking example of one of the important themes of his life: his desire to continue and enhance the policies of his father Dawit.

Under the best of conditions, it is difficult and even reckless to put historical figures 'on the couch' and attribute deep psychological motives to their actions. However, it is difficult to ignore the frequency with which Zär'a Ya'qob invokes his father in the context of his religious reforms. Did this youngest son, who was born with little hope of rising to the throne, shape his life around the vision of his father who died when he was an adolescent? It is certainly interesting to note that he chose the same throne name, Qwäsṭänṭinos (Constantine), as his father. At the least we must concede that on many points the father and son shared a similar vision for their kingdom.

This programme of land grants and church building was directly linked to some of the Ethiopian rulers' earliest contacts with the Christian West, which began with Dawit. Until recently it was widely claimed that the primary purpose of such embassies was to access technical, and particularly military, aid. However, in an important 2021 book, Verena Krebs has demonstrated that such assertions are 'divorced from both source evidence and local historical context' and rooted in a colonialist ideology.[8] In fact, the primary interest of the Ethiopian rulers was in the acquisition of Christian relics, sacred objects and craftsmen (painters and metal-workers) who could produce ecclesiastical works. Dawit acquired relics and reliquaries. In addition, chalices, censers, priestly vestments richly embroidered with religious symbols and biblical scenes, mitres, headbands and girdles came to Ethiopia.

Thus, like their dynasty's putative founder, King Solomon, the Ethiopian rulers sought to enhance their prestige through the lavish gifts they received from around the world. These operated as part of a 'trickle-down' economy in which these gifts found their way to churches and monasteries throughout the land. Dawit's 1402 embassy led to the dispatch of a painter, a metalsmith, two builders and a carpenter to Ethiopia. A quarter of a century later his son Yəsḥaq received thirteen craftsmen from Aragon.

Monthly observances

While the Ethiopian Christian week is organized around the Sabbaths, and as elsewhere in the Christian world different saints are honoured on each day of the year, the Ethiopian Christian calendar also devotes a central place to a series of *monthly* commemorations. Three of these can be traced to similar observances

Manuscript of the *Sənkəssar*, 19th–20th century.

of the Coptic Church, but over the course of time the Ethiopian Church expanded this so that every day is dedicated to the remembrance of Christ, Mary, angels or a saint. Thus the first of each month is dedicated to the birth of Mary, the second to Abba Guba (a rather obscure early Ethiopian saint), the third to the entry of Mary to the Temple, and so on.

The inauguration of many of these recurrent celebrations cannot be precisely dated. The earliest hagiographic manuscripts to contain markings indicating which sections should be read each month in honour of the commemoration of a particular saint date from the sixteenth century. However, several of these observances

Diptych of the Virgin Mary, biblical patriarchs and equestrian saints, 1740–55.

can be directly traced to the calendric reform of Zär'a Ya'qob. His initiation of a monthly celebration of the birth of the Lord is a wonderful example of the multi-levelled character of his religious policies. On or around Christmas Day 1445 he enjoyed a decisive victory over one of the most powerful Muslim rulers of his time, Aḥmad Badläy, who had begun to encroach upon his territory. Zär'a Ya'qob killed his enemy, dismembered him and had his body parts scattered throughout his kingdom.[9]

Zär'a Ya'qob's decision to celebrate the birth of the Lord every month was thus also a de facto commemoration of his military victory. He also composed or commissioned a homiliary known as *Maṣḥafä milad* (Book of the Nativity), which contains readings for each of these monthly observances. In this work he devoted himself not only to the theology of the Trinity and the Incarnation, but inter alia to polemics against his political–religious enemies, including the Stephanites.

Marian devotions

These monthly celebrations were not the only alterations made to the Christian calendar during Zär'a Ya'qob's reign. This can be seen particularly in the realm of Marian piety. In addition to promoting literature and art associated with the Virgin, Zär'a Ya'qob also instituted 33 Marian feasts. Once again, the links between Dawit and Zär'a Ya'qob must be highlighted. According to a well-known tradition, Dawit's queen Ǝgzi' Kəbra dedicated her son Zär'a Ya'qob to Mary when her prayers in her name averted a miscarriage. On the day of his birth, she marked the sign of the cross on his hand in the name of 'Our Lady, the Virgin Mary, Mother of God'.[10]

Two different anaphoras dedicated to the Blessed Virgin were composed during Dawit's reign. One has been tentatively attributed to Samu'el of Waldəbba, an important monastic leader of the time, while the other appears to be the work of Giyorgis of Sägla, one of the Church's most prolific authors. Giyorgis was also the author of *Arganonä maryam* (The Organ of Mary), a voluminous work which contains some of the richest and most moving praises of Mary in Gəʿəz literature.

Over the course of time Dawit and his son came to view Mary not only as their personal intercessor but as the patroness of their dynasty and its hold on power. For his part, Zär'a Ya'qob attributed not only his birth but his rise to the throne to her intervention. Indeed, he chose the Feast of the Dormition ('Ǝräftä) as the date for his coronation. Once again, the overlap between his political and religious motives is noteworthy.

The Virgin and Child with Emperor Dawit II (left) and beginning of a Miracle of Mary (right), from a manuscript of *Tä'ammərä Maryam* (Miracles of Mary), late 15th century.

Maryam Ṣeyon Church, Aksum.

Although at first glance the celebration of Aksum would appear to have little to do with Zär'a Ya'qob's devotion to the cult of Mary, it must be remembered that the city's most important religious site was the cathedral of Aksum-Ṣeyon, which is associated with the Blessed Virgin.[11] Indeed, while the identification of the church with Jerusalem (Ṣeyon) may have taken place at an earlier date, there is considerable evidence that it was during the reign of Zär'a Ya'qob that the identification with Maryam (Mary) solidified. In the prayer that still begins every service the cleric begins by invoking the Trinity and then says, 'I reject you Satan as I stand before this my mother the holy church, which is my witness Mary Zion (Māryām Ṣeyon) forever.'[12]

In the words of Emmanuel Fritsch, one of the foremost experts on the Ethiopian liturgy:

> There is little doubt that this daily confession of faith and abjuration of Satan was created by Zär'a Ya'qob and is his hitherto unidentified Kəḥdatä Säyṭan Abjuration of Satan'. It is also clear that the king was referring there to the church of Mary of Zion at Aksum, adding in the process the name of Mary to the more ancient name of Zion.[13]

'Amdä Ṣəyon moved early in his reign to subdue the rebel Təgrayan governor and claim Solomonic descent for his progeny. However, it was Zär'a Ya'qob who dramatically elevated the prestige of the ancient city. As Bertrand Hirsch and François-Xavier Fauvelle-Aymar have brilliantly shown, it was through his 'ruins policy' that various sites were identified with crucial events in Ethiopian Christian history.[14]

This was also expressed in Zär'a Ya'qob's precedent-setting decision to have his coronation in the city that was the political centre of Təgray province and the spiritual heart of the Church. As we know from his *Ṭomarā təsbə'ət* (Epistle of Humanity), the governor of Təgray had hindered Zär'a Ya'qob's rise to power. It was therefore significant that during his *Šər'atä qʷərḥat* (coronation), the same governor and the head of the church of Aksum-Ṣeyon 'accompanied the king to take him with joy to sacralize his power'.[15]

Cross purposes

Throughout this volume I have referred to the centrality of the Cross as a Christian symbol. I already noted that the conversion of 'Ezana in the fourth century is marked, among other things, by his use of a cross on his coins. The illuminations of the Gärima Gospels depict crosses. As the art historian Claire Bosc-Tiessé proposes, 'Crosses may be the most ancient ceremonial objects in the Christian Aksumite kingdom, as suggested by their depiction on ancient Aksumite coins, [the remains at Yəḥa] and by what is preserved in Zagʷe-era churches.'[16]

According to Jacques Mercier, 'staff-crosses' from sometime between the tenth and the thirteenth century have survived in both Təgray and the Lalibäla regions. Several of these show clear

Processional crosses to be placed on a staff.

affinities with contemporary crosses painted on the walls of the Church of Faras, Nubia, and probably indicate a common origin.[17]

During the Zag^{w}e Period we see dramatic artistic developments in Ethiopian crosses. Processional crosses made of wood, copper, bronze and silver with the cross in an almond- or pear-shaped mandorla or under an arch were particularly widespread. Crosses are often inscribed with additional symbols, including vegetation, the crucified Christ, holy figures (Mary, saints) and animals such as a lamb or ram.

Of all the calendric reforms of the fifteenth century none was as significant and durable as the elevation of Mäsqäl, the Feast of the Finding of the True Cross, to a major celebration in the religio-political year. Although officially a minor feast, it became one of the primary Christian celebrations alongside Easter and Epiphany.[18]

Once again, the seeds of this transformation can be traced to the reign of Dawit. According to several sources, Dawit received a fragment of the True Cross from the Coptic patriarch for securing his freedom when he was imprisoned by the 'King of Egypt'.[19] Whatever our doubts about the historicity of this event, the transformation of Mäsqäl on the seventeenth day, Mäskäräm (27 September), took place if not in the time of Dawit, then certainly by the reign of his son, Zär'a Ya'qob.

Procession of priests and deacons during Təmqät (Epiphany) celebrations, Jinka.

The timing of this festival is also of great significance. The 'winter' months of June to August in Ethiopia are the rainy season (*kərämt*). Thus the ability of an emperor, or in some cases a local ruler, to gather the resources for a great feast in late September was an expression not only of piety but of his control of resources.[20] This was further strengthened by the summoning of local vassals to the royal court, where their appointments were made, improved, diminished or cancelled. A ritual procession around a bonfire (*dämära*) took place in a strict hierarchical order, while mock combat between soldiers from different regions (mimicked today in a 'battle-of-the bands' competition between parish choirs) all stressed the instability of rivalries.

Just as with the veneration of Mary, the Cross was promoted not only through literature and feasts, but through expressive culture. However, only in this later period did the practice of affixing a cross on royal dwellings originate. According to his chronicler, Zär'a Ya'qob had a gold cross placed on the roof of his palace at Däbrä Bərhan, setting this precedent. By his command the sign of the Cross was affixed to the belongings of Christians, including clothes, weapons and ploughs. Indeed, the Cross became the literal embodiment of Christian identity, as believers were expected to tattoo the sign of the Cross on their hands and foreheads.

This tattooing and branding of the Cross seems also to have been associated with the Christian custom of wearing a *matäb*: 'a cord twisted of three different colours (to symbolize the Trinity)'.[21] The cord became one of the most important signifiers of Christian identity. Usually, a small cross was hung on it. The Portuguese reported, 'All the priests, monks and lords carry crosses in their hand, both on foot and on horseback; and the laymen of the commonality and lower people carry little crosses round their necks.'[22]

However, the Cross was far more than the company logo of Christianity. It possessed a remarkable power which manifested itself for the benefit of believers and to the chagrin of their enemies. Märha (Yəmərḥannä) Krəstos, for many years the abbot of the important monastery of Däbrä Libanos, and a contemporary of Zär'a Ya'qob, met a man who was possessed by a demon. He made

Preparations for Mäsqäl feast, 2018.

Woman adorned with crosses, 1993.

the sign of the Cross and the demon fled. On another occasion he healed a woman infested by snakes by giving her water in which he had washed the cross.

Icons

Dawit and Zär'a Ya'qob's reigns are also visually significant because of the emergence of the painting of icons. The term *śəʿəl* ('image') refers to both three-dimensional and two-dimensional images. Illumination of manuscripts dates to the Aksumite Period with the Gärima Gospels. However, the practice of painting portraits of saints on portable wooden panels emerges in the first half of the fifteenth century. While the importation of Byzantine icons probably had some role, the development seems to have gone hand in hand with the development of the cult of Mary. Both Dawit and Zär'a Ya'qob are specifically mentioned as having cherished her image, with the latter mandating its devotion in every church and on all her feast days.

In Ethiopia as elsewhere, icons were not merely to be seen but to be experienced. Not only did believers gaze upon, prostrate

Canon table from the Gärima Gospels, *c.* 530–660.

The Magi and the shepherds, leaf from an illuminated Gospel manuscript from the Stephanite Monastery at Gundä Gunde, first half of the 16th century.

themselves before and pray to icons, but the icons themselves watched, acted and responded. In the words of a miracle of Mary, which probably dates from the period of Zä'ra Ya'qob, the

> icon is clothed with a (human) body. It moves and talks. The Spirit of God dwells in it. You should not think it is a (mere) picture. She is, indeed, Our Lady the Virgin (herself) and he is Jesus, the Only-Begotten Son himself. Mika'el and Gäbrə'el, too, are as themselves.[23]

Believers, moreover, did not have to enter a church to encounter the picture of the Virgin. Devotees commonly wore her image around their necks.

Not surprisingly, the reforms and innovations imposed by Zä'ra Ya'qob provoked a fair amount of opposition. While he had made moves to placate the disciples of Täklä Haymanot and raised the status of his home monastery of Däbrä (Asbo) Libanos, he shrewdly judged that they had become too comfortable as beneficiaries of royal generosity to revolt. For the more recalcitrant and independent Ewosṭatians, the decision on their behalf in the Sabbath controversy and various other concessions tempered their anger. Moreover, by assigning them to minister in areas far from the regions where they had the strongest spiritual and political support, he made it easier to divide their loyalties.

A much thornier problem was yet another radical monastic movement which emerged in some of the most inaccessible regions of the Agame region of eastern Təgray. Founded by Abba Sämu'el of Däbrä Qwäyäṣa, a widely respected monastic leader, under the leadership of Əsṭifanos it became an extreme ascetic movement, cut off from the outside world. Most importantly, the Əsṭifanosites (Stephanites) rejected the emperor's right to make major changes in Christian ritual and particularly opposed his innovations that glorified the Blessed Virgin and Christ. While these monks probably saw themselves as bulwarks fighting against the attempts of a lay ruler to reshape the Church, Zä'ra Ya'qob saw them as rebel clerics who attacked the king and the state. He had them tortured and imprisoned and, in some cases, executed.

It must be noted here that, for all his successes, Zä'ra Ya'qob was a ruthless ruler who governed his kingdom with an iron fist. He was constantly seeking out and discovering enemies. Some were accused of supernatural crimes such as magic, sorcery and consulting with demons. Others were charged with nefarious political plots to overthrow the king or at the very least weaken him. As his power grew, the number of courtiers he could depend upon shrank. He replaced local officials with members of his own family or others of untarnished loyalty. Not surprisingly, a system that relied on the power of one man, and the fear of his wrath, was difficult to maintain after his death.

Gə'əz literature

Throughout much of this volume I have made note of various works of Gə'əz literature. Now, however, is the opportunity to offer a more focused survey. The past fifty years have seen a revolution in the ease with which scholars can access manuscripts. This has resulted in both the discovery of new works and the preparation of more complete editions of previously published texts. Unfortunately, there has yet to be a comprehensive work documenting this progress. No scholar has attempted to produce a book-length history of Gə'əz literature since 1968, and even this work was a revision of an earlier (1956, 1961) publication.[24] Thus a considerable gap has developed between our knowledge of individual works in Ethiopic literature and our overall understanding of the development of the corpus. Moreover, even in the existing surveys, articles and monographs the emphasis has been more literary and text-critical than historical. Thus we often know more about the manuscripts that have been preserved than we do about the general trends of cultural interaction, transmission and revision.[25]

From the thirteenth to the eighteenth century dozens of works were translated from Arabic into Gə'əz. So numerous are these works that no complete list of them has been compiled.[26] There is, however, no question that translations from Arabic transformed the corpus of Ethiopian Christian literature. Theological issues were redefined, and the Alexandrian position was articulated with ever greater clarity. In the process of translation, moreover, the Gəʿəz language itself was transformed on both the lexical and syntactical levels through the introduction of new roots and an enlarged range of the meanings of existing roots.

I would be remiss if I did not comment on the fact that this enormous flourishing of translations began almost a thousand years after the initial acceptance of Christianity in Ethiopia. It is difficult to think of any other church in which so many 'foreign' works have been added to the body of religious literature at so late a date in its history. Here, as elsewhere, the comparative fluidity that characterized Ethiopian Christianity throughout much of its history is worthy of mention. The introduction of so many new literary works must be seen alongside innovations in the liturgical calendar, cultic practice and many other aspects of Church life.

Although we cannot rule out individual translations under 'private' auspices, in at least one case in Egypt and not in Ethiopia, this must have been the exception rather than the rule. The number of Ethiopian clerics literate in Arabic must have been small, and the number of Copts who resided in Ethiopia long enough to master Gəʿəz perhaps even smaller. Inevitably, these two groupings were clustered around the court or Ethiopia's major monasteries, where they probably worked in tandem on translations. Moreover, given the size of some of the works translated and the sheer quantity of these translations, only those who commanded significant resources could afford to undertake a project or projects of this magnitude. Indeed, as we shall see, a relatively small number of metropolitans, emperors and monastic leaders appear to have been behind a disproportionate number of translations.

Best remembered among these Egyptian clerics was Abunä Sälama, 'the Translator'; he was both a patron of translation and an active translator himself. During his incumbency as head of the Church from 1348 to 1388, Arabic literature had an enormous influence on Ethiopic literature. Abunä Sälama is closely associated with one of the major literary projects of this period: the revision of the existing translation of the Bible based on an Arabic *Vorlage*. In the *Sənkəssar* (Calendar of the Saints) his death is commemorated by the following poetic reading:

On this day died Abba Salama, the translator
Greetings to you, root of the tree of the faith
Upon whom the commandments of the Law and the Gospels have been poured Salama, how your memory has abided with us!
By your lips sweeter than the scent of myrrh and aloe
Have the Scriptures been translated from Arabic into Ge'ez.[27]

Despite this tradition that the Scriptures were translated from Arabic during this period, most scholars agree that we are not dealing here with a completely new translation, but rather with a re-editing of the existing text. In contrast to the initial translation of the Bible from Greek, which appears to have been unsystematic and taken place over decades, if not centuries, this revised text was better coordinated and took far less time to reach fruition.

Some of the texts that reached Ethiopia from the fourteenth century on were not original compositions of the Coptic Church. At least a handful of translations appear to be 'connected to Sinai rather than Egypt, represented by texts like the *Acts of Arethas* (*Gädlä Ḫirut*), the *Acts of Kaleb* (*Gädlä Kaleb*), the *Acts of Athanasius of Clysma* and the *Acts of Azqir* (*Gädlä Azqir*), that have no parallel in Coptic Arabic literature'.[28] Indeed, translations from Arabic proved to be a vital conduit of material from diverse traditions into Gəʿəz literature. Particularly noteworthy in this context are works that are attributed to Syrian Orthodox Church fathers, including Ephrem (d. 373), James of Sarugh (d. 521) and John Saba (d. *c.* 780).[29] It is interesting to note also that in several cases, such as *Motä Aron* (The Death of Aaron), *Dərsanä sänbät* (Homily on the Sabbath) and *Dərsanä Abrəham wäSəra bägəbs* (Homily on Abraham and Sarah in Egypt), works are attributed to these authors. Moreover, in all three of these cases (and several others) these works were eventually adopted by the Betä Ǝsra'el.

Translation was also not the end of the process in the case of works that, while originally based upon Arabic originals, were adapted and revised for use in the Ethiopian Church. Of the numerous works translated from Arabic over the centuries, special mention should be made of two: *Täʾammərä Maryam* (Miracles of Mary) and the *Sənkəssar* (Synaxarium; Calendar of the Saints) both massive works whose translation was initiated under the patronage of Emperor Dawit.

The *Sənkəssar* is a collection of short biographies of the saints arranged according to the days of the year. It is a calendar of the saints, martyrs and angels in which each is commemorated on a specific day (usually of his/her death) or days. The passages from the *Sənkəssar* are read in church each day as part of the service.

The Arabic version of the *Sənkəssar* was compiled in the thirteenth century and made extensive use of Coptic Church sources. More than a century later, in the late fourteenth or early fifteenth century, a monk in the Egyptian monastery of St Antony translated the work into Gə'əz. Although doubtless a welcome addition to the Ethiopic literature on the saints, as a simple translation the *Sənkəssar* was in a sense deeply flawed, because it did not contain information on local saints. Over the course of time, Ethiopian authors worked enthusiastically to remedy this lacuna as they added material that indigenized the text. Indeed, since the editing and revision of the texts took place on a local basis rather than through any centralized or unified initiative, different manuscripts came to reflect the interests of a specific monastery or religious movement. However, between 1563 and 1581 a major revision was undertaken, probably at Däbrä Ḥayq, only to be rivalled a few decades later at Däbrä Libanos.

The *Tä'ammərä Maryam* (Miracles of Mary) is yet another example in which translation from Arabic should be viewed as the beginning of a literary process rather than its culmination. The text that reached Ethiopia included miracles that had originated in Spain, France, Palestine and particularly Egypt. However, as with the *Sənkəssar*, Ethiopian Christians did not limit themselves to the passive reception of tales that originated in distant lands. New miracles recording local appearances of the Virgin were soon added to the text. Over the course of time the collection grew to include more than a thousand miracle stories.[30]

Although it might be tempting to assume that translations were solely the work of the Egyptian abun and his Ethiopian allies, the testimony of the literature reveals a far more complicated picture. This can best be illustrated by an examination of the career of the outstanding Ethiopian author of the late fourteenth and early fifteenth centuries, the monk known as Giyorgis of Sägla. He is also one of the few Ethiopian authors whom we can clearly identify and hence construct their literary biography.[31] Moreover, his activities warn against simplistic distinctions between authors and translators or pro-Alexandrians and their opponents.

Born into a family of court clerics, Giyorgis of Sägla was educated at Iyäsus Mo'a's great monastery of Däbrä Ḥayq Ǝsṭifanos. Here he was able to benefit from both access to its magnificent library and travel to other communities, and thus had unparalleled exposure to the literature of his time. This is particularly evident in his authorship of the *Mäṣḥafä məśṭir* (Book of the Mystery), a significant theological work that displays his great knowledge of the most important works not only of his time, but of the Aksumite Period.

His prayer for the breaking (of the bread) was a eucharistic prayer or anaphora written at the instigation of the Egyptian Abuna Bärtälomewos. Although the composition of the text at the behest of the metropolitan might be interpreted as an indication that Giyorgis was pro-Egyptian in his orientation, his position vis-à-vis the Coptic Church appears more complex. Giyorgis was, for example, one of the major supporters of the pro-Sabbath position (bitterly opposed by the same Bärtälomewos), and he composed several prayers and homilies on this theme, including in all probability the Anaphora of Athanasius.

Giyorgis is also remembered, moreover, as the author of the *Mäṣḥafä säʿatat* (Hours of Prayers). This work was composed to replace the Coptic schedule of prayers then in use. To further complicate the picture, he is also credited in some traditions with the translation of the Athanasian Creed into Gəʿəz. Thus a single author can be seen to have opposed the abun on the subject of the Sabbath, cooperated with him in the composition of a prayer, composed a major liturgical work to replace Coptic examples, and translated a doctrinal document treasured by the Copts.

No discussion of Ethiopian literature during the fifteenth century would be complete without a discussion of the works attributed to Zär'a Ya'qob. While it is impossible to determine whether these works were composed by the king himself or under his patronage in a royal scriptorium, they are an important source for the religious controversies of his time. I have mentioned several of them already in this chapter.

Ǝgzi'abəḥer nägśä (The Lord Reigns) are hymns devoted to saints, Mary, the Trinity and the Sabbaths.[32] *Mäṣḥafä bərhan* (The Book of Light) is an extensive collection of homilies advocating for Zär'a Ya'qob's ecclesiastic reforms, including the first Sabbath, the sign of the Cross and the mätäb. *Mäṣḥafä baḥrəy* (The Book of the Pearl/Essence) encapsulates his campaign against 'magic'; *Mäṣḥafä milad* (The Book of the Nativity) was read on the monthly celebrations of the Incarnation, Christ's birth, and attacks both the *ayhud* (Jews) who rejected the Trinity and the Ǝsṭifanosites. *Ṭomarä təsbə'ət* (The Epistle of Humanity) is a collection of three homilies to be read in honour of the Apostles and Evangelists which offers strong condemnations of various types of sorcerers, magicians, soothsayers and demons.

Prior to the reign of Zär'a Ya'qob, Ethiopian rulers and those around them did not record 'chronicles' of their reigns.[33] As I noted in the previous chapter, the account of the 'Wars' of 'Amdä Ṣəyon is not a chronicle and many scholars believe that even if it contains elements that are contemporaneous with his reign, the finished work dates to the fifteenth or even sixteenth century.

Zär'a Ya'qob's chronicle is, in fact, a combination of two previously independent works that offer slightly different perspectives on his reign. One was composed by his contemporaries, although apparently not under his auspices; the other probably dates to half a century later. This marks a new tradition in the composition of indigenous historiography.

This period also saw the flowering of hagiographic literature. The 'Life' of P̣änṭälewon, who is said to have lived during the reign of Kaleb, is preserved in a manuscript from the time of Dawit. He is the first of the Nine Saints to be thus commemorated. Two versions of the Life of Täklä Haymanot were composed in the first half of the fifteenth century, with yet another dating to about a century later. The 'Life' of Filəp̣pos, the third abbot of Däbrä

Libanos, was composed circa 1425 at the same time as the *gädlat* (life) of his contemporaries Bäṣalotä Mikaʾel and Anorewos. This is also the period of the composition of the Lives of Lalibäla and Yəmrəḥannä Krestos, Zagʷe rulers.[34]

In the context of our discussion of these hagiographic texts it must be noted that the Ethiopian Church has never had a centralized process of canonization like that which developed among Catholics during the twelfth century. While the eventual inclusion of a saint into the 'canonical/national' version of the *Sənkəssar* was an achievement, many saints were venerated on a local level, with their 'Life' being composed and read only in their home monastery or those closely associated with it. In fact, such a local saint might be remembered only in this 'native' calendar of the saints.

Another hagio-liturgical innovation that may date to the middle of the fifteenth century is the hymnographic genre known as *mälkəʾ* (image or effigy), in which the saint's body, the path from conception to death, and monastic garments are praised.[35] Although the earliest manuscript records of this genre date to the seventeenth century, Zärʾa Yaʿqob and his son and successor Bäʾədä Maryam are both credited with authoring works of this type.

External affairs

Dawit and Yəṣḥaq both continued the struggles with Ifat which began under earlier rulers. Dawit sustained victories against both Ḥaqq al-Dīn II (d. 1386) and his brother and successor Saʿd al-Dīn II (d. 1415?). The latter sought sanctuary in Zaylaʿ, but was eventually killed there. Shortly thereafter Yəshaq conquered this port city and ended the sovereignty of the Sultanate of Ifat.

The surviving members of the dynasty took refuge in Yemen, and when they returned to their homeland they continued the struggle through the Sultanate of ʿAdal (Barr Saʿd al-Din), which was less exposed to Christian attacks. They were no more successful in their opposition to the Christian kingdom from this new base, as successive rulers were defeated by their rivals. Indeed, as I noted above, Aḥmad Badläy, who was disparagingly called Arwe (snake) Badlāy, was defeated by Zärʾa Yaʿqob, shattering the sultanate.

This powerful victory must be understood against the background of yet another innovation, one which appears to date to the time of Zär'a Ya'qob. Under his leadership, the army was reorganized around royal troops (*ḉäwa*), who were military corps associated with the king's court and not dependent on local governors.[36]

Continuing with the theme of Islam, the urban settlement of Harlaa, which I discussed briefly in Chapter Five, declined dramatically in the fifteenth century. This may have been related to recurrent episodes of plague both in its Egyptian trading partner and in Ethiopia itself.[37] Water stress, warfare and population migration were probably also important factors. The foundation in the early sixteenth century of Harar, which would become the most important Muslim town in the Horn, would appear to support the last of these.[38]

Muslim submission to the dictates of the Christian kingdom was of importance not only for the external relations of the sultanates, but for the major effect it had on their internal politics. While establishment forces, political leaders and their clerical allies were willing to accept accommodation to the dictates of their Christian overlords, there were always groups who opposed these Christian–Muslim accommodations. It must always be remembered that an increase in education, pilgrimage and contacts with more radical Muslims from the religion's heartland could always influence local populations.

Despite the long history of Christianity in Ethiopia, the last decades of the fourteenth century and most of the fifteenth century mark an important formative period in the history of this religion. Changes in the rhythm, practice, representation and performance of the faith led to deep transformations in Christian life. Although often presented as antique elements which dated to the early days of Ethiopian Christianity, many of these can be firmly dated to the medieval period.

EPILOGUE

Since the publication of Taddesse Tamrat's *Church and State in Ethiopia*, scholars have viewed the period from 1478 to 1527 as one of decline.[1] However, this view has recently been challenged by Verena Krebs, who sees it as a period of prosperity.[2] Whatever our verdict, it is clear that important changes took place in the first decades of the sixteenth century.

The beginning of the sixteenth century did not, of course, suddenly usher in a dramatic new period in Ethiopian history. There is ample continuity between this period and the previous centuries. However, there are important justifications on the local, regional and global levels to conclude my narrative in around 1500. The incursion of militant Muslims, the Ottoman assertion of control of the Red Sea, the arrival of the first Europeans and the expansion of the Oromo each introduced new forces into the maelstrom of Ethiopian history. A discussion of any of these topics would require me to provide vast amounts of background material and detailed discussions of factors that have not previously been treated in this book. Moreover, in the context of a discussion of 'lost civilizations' there can be little question that the term no longer applies to Ethiopian civilizations.

Militant Islam

Scholars have for many years speculated as to why the Christian kingdom of Ethiopia was not conquered during the first dramatic expansion of Islam as it swept across North Africa and the Middle

East. Even as Muslims became a dominant political force in the Mediterranean, Red Sea and Indian Ocean trade, the Ethiopian plateau remained under Christian sovereignty. As I noted in Chapter Four, there is a tradition that because of the hospitality that the *nağāšī* offered Muhammed's early followers, Ethiopia was explicitly spared from conquest and political domination. It is, however, far more likely that this tradition is an ex post facto justification. The division of labour between Muslim traders and pastoralists on the one hand, and Christian overlords and agriculturalists on the other, was mutually beneficial. Certainly, throughout much of their history the Christian emperors valued tribute and political obeisance over the demands of conversion. In the Horn of Africa, as in many other places, Muslim leaders proved adept in finding ways to accommodate the demands of *sharia* law to the realities of everyday life.

However, a variety of internal and external factors led to a crisis of leadership in the Muslim principalities of the Horn of Africa. The most dramatic expression of this was the jihad led by Aḥmad b. Ibrāhīm al Ġāzī, commonly known as Aḥmad Gragn (Grañ), 'the left-handed'. Social tensions, economic problems and contact with more radical visions of Islam all probably played a role. Unfortunately, given the limits of our sources, we are, to a considerable degree, reading these factors retroactively back into the jihad. Nevertheless, there can be little question that, by the end of the fifteenth century, the political establishment in the Muslim principalities was seriously undermined by prophetic *amir*s (princes/rulers). Scholars of Islam in Africa have documented similar patterns elsewhere in Africa and far beyond.[3]

While Gragn and his forces were ultimately defeated, they changed the dynamic between Christianity and Islam in the Horn. Not only were vast quantities of Christian wealth destroyed, but the expansive activities of the Solomonic rulers were stymied. Islam was much more securely established within the Christian polity, ushering in a new period in Christian–Muslim relations.

The Ottoman Red Sea

In 1516 the Ottoman Empire, under the leadership of Sultan Selim I (r. 1512–20), conquered Mamluk Egypt.[4] The Ottoman involvement in the region seems to have been motivated by a combination of factors, including their rivalry with the Portuguese (see below) and a desire to present themselves as the champions of Islam in the region. The Ottomans inherited from the Mamluks the position of being the protectors of the two holy cities of Mecca and Medina, which would in subsequent years form one of the most important means by which the Ottoman relationship with the Indian Ocean world was mediated, both through the pilgrimage and through the credibility that control of the shrines gave to Ottoman, universally recognized, Muslim rulers. However, for much of the sixteenth century, Ottoman involvement in the Indian Ocean continued to revolve around the threat presented by the Portuguese. As had been the case throughout much of history, control of the Red Sea was intimately connected to the spice trade and the control of routes to India.

The Oromo

For many years scholars of Ethiopia adopted a view of Ethiopian history that was in keeping with the dominant political ideology of the imperial period. In keeping with this 'Church and state' perspective, the establishment of churches and the rise and fall of successive monarchs provided the framework for the reconstruction of history. Peoples, such as the pastoral Oromo (usually referred to by the derogatory term 'Galla' (infidels, 'pagans')), were viewed as invaders, or at least newcomers. Thus in 1973, in the fourth edition of *The Ethiopians*, Edward Ullendorff dismissed the importance of the Oromo, saying, 'The Gallas had little to contribute to the Semiticized civilization of Ethiopia, they possessed no significant material or intellectual culture . . . They were not the only cause of the depressed state into which the country now sank, but they helped to prolong a situation.'[5] Curiously, when these words were published the first major political changes in Ethiopia had already begun.[6]

Over the past half-century major strides have been taken to rectify this situation. Although it is sometimes difficult to disentangle these new scholarly voices from the painful political conflicts of the post-imperial period, there is little question that the full history of Ethiopia, particularly from the end of the fifteenth century onwards, cannot be written without a detailed discussion of the Oromo. They are the single largest ethnic group in the country. For the purposes of this volume, the exploration of their origins, socio-political structure and economic lives would take me deeply into a new set of issues, institutions and controversies, and so I have not attempted it.[7]

The Portuguese

The end of the fifteenth century marked a radical turning point in relations between Christian Europe and the rest of the world. Hand in hand, mercantile fleets and Catholic missionaries set out to explore recently 'discovered' parts of the world. It is often forgotten that the tiny country of Portugal was the first European power to extend its political influence into Africa. Although some scholars have bemoaned the lack of interest in pre-colonial Africa in recent years,[8] this is certainly not the case regarding the Portuguese and Jesuit encounter with Ethiopia. In the past two decades there has been a flowering of research on all aspects of this early European presence, including religion, art, archaeology and politics.[9]

From the perspective of this volume the Portuguese arrival was significant because it represents the emergence of a new and important body of literature on Ethiopia and the Horn. Although many of the features which the European authors describe were of relatively recent vintage and dated to the middle or last half of the fifteenth century, these newcomers had no way to know this. Not only did they accept the antiquity of much of what they observed, but this perspective was adopted by future generations in reconstructing the Ethiopian past. Much of the recent scholarship I quote above has been devoted to revising this perspective. For all these reasons, it is appropriate to conclude this book in around 1500.

For almost half a century I have devoted my academic career to research and teaching on African history in general and specifically on Ethiopia. As I completed this volume, I could not help but note that in many places what I have written in this book revises, challenges and even contradicts claims I put forward in my earlier works. While it is somewhat troubling to have been 'wrong' in my assumptions, it is gratifying to see the way in which scholarship has built on earlier works and moved in new directions.

Given the wonderful flowering of research on ancient and medieval Ethiopia in recent years, I would be naive if I thought that this volume would have a long history as a definitive work.[10] Rather, I prefer to view it as a timely intervention in an ongoing historical conversation.

For readers for whom this volume marks their first introduction to the panorama of Ethiopian history, I hope that I have succeeded in balancing clarity and complexity. For those for whom the pages above mark a serious revision of their previous understanding of Ethiopian history, I hope they are accepted with the seriousness and respect with which they are intended. I am well aware that some readers may find many of my claims surprising and troubling. This is not the first time I have written a book that upends previously held views.[11] I am deeply aware that all too often the examination of the distant past is read as a commentary on the present and future. It is my sincerest hope that what I have written will prove interesting to general readers and encourage specialists to consider my arguments and challenge my views.

REFERENCES

References to Ethiopian personal names are listed as is customary in Ethiopia with the personal name and the name of the father in that order. Succeeding references are as, for example, Taddesse Tamrat, further listed as Taddesse, not as Tamrat, since Tamrat is *not* a family name.

PROLOGUE

1 Norman Juster, *The Phantom Tollbooth* (New York, 1961), p. 9.

2 'The Food Wife', *The Simpsons*, Season 23, Episode 5, 13 November 2011.

3 Christine Sciacca's important volume *Ethiopia at the Crossroads*, exh. cat., Walters Art Museum, Baltimore, MD (New Haven, CT, and London, 2024), appeared too late for its discussions to be integrated into this book.

4 Jack Goody, *Cooking, Cuisine and Class: A Study in Comparative Sociology* (Cambridge, 1982), p. 210, also p. 213.

5 Sarah F. Derbew, *Untangling Blackness in Greek Antiquity* (Cambridge, 2022), p. 13, emphasis in original. Derbew is here referencing the important African American scholar W.E.B. Du Bois; see her reference n. 39.

6 Verena Krebs and Yonatan Binyam, *'Ethiopia' and the World, 330–1500* (Cambridge, 2024).

7 Getachew Metaferia, 'Ethiopia: A Bulwark against European Colonialism and Its Role in the Pan-African Movement', in *The Battle of Adwa: Reflections on Ethiopia's Historic Victory against European Colonialism*, ed. Paulos Milkias and Getachew Metaferia (Kanata, ON, 2005), pp. 181–216.

8 Erin C. MacLeod, *Visions of Zion: Ethiopians and Rastafari in the Search for the Promised Land* (New York, 2014); Giulia Bonacci, 'The Irresistible Ascent of Rās Tafari in the Black Imagination', *Annales d'Éthiopie*, XVIII/1 (2013), pp. 395–7.

9 Haile Selassie's address to the United Nations, 1963, available at https://digitallibrary.un.org, accessed 27 January 2025.

10 Here as elsewhere I rely upon the Revised Standard Version (American) English translation of the Bible.

11 Yehuda T. Radday, 'The Four Rivers of Paradise', *Hebrew Studies*, XXXII (1982), pp. 23–31.

12 See Sarah M. Schellinger, *Nubia* (London, 2022), for a detailed discussion of this region.

13 J.R.R. Tolkien, 'Sigelwara Land', *Medium Aevum*, I/3 (1932), pp. 183–96; III/2 (1934), pp. 95–111, esp. 107. For the rather far-fetched theory that

Tolkien's work was broadly inspired by Ethiopia see Michael Muhling, *The Real Middle-Earth: Discovering the Origin of 'The Lord of the Rings'* (Glen Waverley, Vic., 2003).

14 For a fascinating recent analysis of the treatment of Black skin colour in Greek literature and the visual culture of antiquity see Derbew, *Untangling Blackness*.

15 Adam Simmons, *Nubia, Ethiopia, and the Crusading World, 1095–1402* (London, 2022).

16 For a valuable survey see the volume in the same series (Lost Civilizations) as this book: Andrew Robinson, *The Indus* (London, 2021).

17 Samantha Kelly, *Translating Faith: Ethiopian Pilgrims in Renaissance Rome* (Cambridge, MA, 2024).

18 Pierre Schneider, *L'Éthiopie et l'Inde: Interférences et confusions aux extrémités du monde antique (VIIIe siècle avant JC–VIe siècle après JC)*, Collections de l'École française de Rome, CCCV (Rome, 2004); and Pierre Schneider, 'The So-Called Confusion between India and Ethiopia: The Eastern and Southern Edges of the Inhabited World from the Greco-Roman Perspective', in *Brill's Companion to Ancient Geography*, ed. Serena Bianchetti, Michelle R. Cataudella and Hans-Joachim Gehrke (Leiden and Boston, MA, 2016), pp. 184–202. It is interesting, if not definitive, to note that the Gəʿəz term for an elephant, *näge*, may be traceable to the Sanskrit *nāga*.

19 Recently, Wendy Belcher of Princeton University has suggested that the term 'Habesha' be used to designate 'the people of the Ethiopian highlands (modern-day Ethiopia and Eritrea) who have traditionally written in the Afro-Asiatic language of **ግዕዝ** (Gəʿəz)and speak modern languages descended from Ge'ez.' Wendy Laura Belcher, *Abyssinia's Samuel Johnson: Ethiopian Thought in the Making of an English Author* (Oxford, 2012), p. 19.

20 Edward Ullendorff, *The Ethiopians: An Introduction to Country and People* (Oxford, 1960, and numerous later editions); Richard Pankhurst, *The Ethiopians: A History* (Oxford, 1998).

21 Christopher Clapham, review of Richard Pankhurst's *The Ethiopians* in the *Times Literary Supplement*, 7 May 1999. I am grateful to Professor Clapham for providing me with a copy of his review.

22 Simmons, *Nubia, Ethiopia, and the Crusading World*, p. 21. Much of the debate here revolves around the precise meaning of 'Ethiopians' in early Aksumite inscriptions.

23 Christina Riggs, *Egypt* (London, 2017), pp. 44–5, 141–51.

24 Edward Gibbon, *The History of the Decline and Fall of the Roman Empire*, Chapter XLII, Part IV, p. 92, available at https://ccel.org. It must also be noted that northern Ethiopians do not consider themselves to be black (Amharic: *ṭəqur*), but rather reddish-brown (Amharic: *qäyy*). For them, black people are those who live in the Sudan, Kenya and southern Ethiopia. Thus when they travel outside Ethiopia it is often a shock to Ethiopians that outsiders do not distinguish them from these Black Africans.

25 Carlo Conti Rossini, *Storia d'Etiopia*, part I: *Delle origini all'avvento della dinastia salomonide* (Milan, 1928), pp. 91–106. See Ullendorff, *The Ethiopians*, p. 51: 'Numerically the South Arabian leaven was not significant, but its *superior quality* revolutionized life in the Abyssinian highlands' (emphasis added).

26 Stuart Munro-Hay, *Aksum: An African Civilisation of Late Antiquity* (Edinburgh, 1991); David W. Phillipson, *Foundations of an African Civilisation: Aksum and the Northern Horn, 1000 BC–AD 1300* (Oxford, 2012).

27 Quoted in Munro-Hay, *Aksum*, p. 17.

28 Gibbon, *Decline and Fall*, Chapter Forty-Seven, Part VI, p. 156. Of course, it must be noted that 'the world' of which Gibbon wrote was very circumscribed and limited to Europe and the Mediterranean basin.

29 Simmons, *Nubia, Ethiopia, and the Crusading World*, p. 45. See Ephraim Isaac, *The Ethiopian Orthodox Täwahïdo Church* (Trenton, NJ, 2012), p. 22: 'From the beginning of the seventh century to the end of the thirteenth, very little is known of the history of the Ethiopian Orthodox Tewahedo Church.' Ullendorff, *The Ethiopians*, p. 2: 'But from the threshold to the close of the Middle Ages Ethiopia was far removed from the view of the outside world and lived in an isolation which was tumultuous rather than splendid.'

30 Harold Marcus, *A History of Ethiopia* (Berkeley and Los Angeles, CA, and London, 1994), pp. 1–29; Paul B. Henze, *Layers of Time: A History of Ethiopia* (New York, 2002), pp. 1–82; Saheed A. Adejumobi, *The History of Ethiopia* (Westport, CT, and London, 2007), pp. 1–22.

31 Belcher, *Abyssinia's Samuel Johnson*, p. 23: 'An Ethiopian friend once joked that no matter what question you ask an Ethiopian the answer always begins, "Well, three thousand years ago . . . "'. Countless discussions of the history of the Bətä Əsra'el (Ethiopian Jews) claim that their presence in Ethiopia dates back at least 2,000 years.

32 James C. McCann, *Stirring the Pot: A History of African Cuisine* (Athens, OH, 2009), p. 80, and see also pp. 58–61.

33 Hiroki Ishikawa, 'Increase in Teff Consumption in Northern Ethiopia between the 16th and 18th Centuries and the Birth of Injera', *African Study Monographs: Supplementary Issue*, LXI (2023), pp. 7–40. I will leave it to specialists in agricultural history to evaluate this suggestion.

34 Rita Pankhurst, 'The Coffee Ceremony and the History of Coffee Consumption in Ethiopia', in *Ethiopia in Broader Perspective (Kyoto, 12–17 December 1997)*, vol. II, ed. Katsuyoshi Fukui, Eisei Kurimoto and Masayoshi Shigeta (Kyoto, 1997), pp. 516–39.

35 Aaron Michael Butts, 'Mind the Gap: Sources for Late Antique Aksum' is currently in preparation. An oral version of this paper was delivered at Princeton University, 9 March 2020.

36 Marie-Laure Derat, *L'Énigme d'une dynastie sainte et usurpatrice dans le royaume chrétien d'Éthiopie du XIe au XIIIe siècle* (Turnhout, 2018).

37 Marcus, 'The Golden Age of the Solomonic Dynasty to 1500', in his *History of Ethiopia*, pp. 17–29; Jacques Mercier, *Art of Ethiopia: From the Origins to the Golden Century* (Paris, 2021), pp. 131–296.
38 This latter term was first suggested to me in a conversation with Dr Getatchew Haile.
39 Steven Kaplan, *Les Falâshâs* (Maredsous, 1990).
40 Steven Kaplan, *The Beta Israel (Falasha) in Ethiopia: From Earliest Times to the Twentieth Century* (New York, 1992).
41 Alessandro Bausi, 'Writing, Copying, Translating: Ethiopia as a Manuscript Culture', in *Manuscript Cultures: Mapping the Field*, vol. I, ed. Jörg Quenzer, Dmitry Bondarev and Jan-Ulrich Sobisch (Berlin, Munich and Boston, MA, 2014), pp. 37–78.
42 Niall Finneran, *The Archaeology of Ethiopia* (London and New York, 2007).
43 Timothy Insoll, 'Ethiopia and the Horn of Africa', in *The Oxford Handbook of Islamic Archaeology*, ed. Bethany J. Walker, Timothy Insoll and Corisande Fenwick (Oxford, 2020), pp. 417–45.

1 THE MANY FACES OF THE QUEEN OF SHEBA

1 Catherine Hickley, 'Queen of Sheba's Palace Discovered in Ethiopia', http://ethiopianreview.com, 11 May 2008.
2 Siegbert Uhlig, 'Did Helmut Ziegert Discover the Queen of Sheba's Palace?', www.aai.uni-hamburg.de, 10 May 2008.
3 Dalya Alberge, 'Archaeologists Strike Gold in Quest to Find Queen of Sheba's Wealth', *The Guardian*, www.theguardian.com, 12 February 2012.
4 Helen Briggs, 'DNA Clues to Queen of Sheba Tale', www.bbc.com, 21 June 2012.
5 Stanley Stewart, 'In Search of the Real Queen of Sheba', www.nationalgeographic.co.uk, 5 December 2018.
6 See 'Searching for the Queen of Sheba', www.bbc.co.uk/news, 31 May 1999.
7 *The Testament of Solomon*, trans. F. C. Conybeare, pdf formatted by P. Yardley, at www.tonyburke.ca, accessed 1 July 2022.
8 Jacob Lassner, *Demonizing the Queen of Sheba: Boundaries of Gender and Culture in Postbiblical Judaism and Medieval Islam* (Chicago, IL, 1993).
9 Kristen Collins and Bryan C. Keene, eds, *Balthazar: A Black African King in Medieval and Renaissance Art* (Los Angeles, CA, 2023).
10 Berry was born to an African American father and a (White) English German mother. Some sources, however, identify her as simply African American.
11 Stuart Munro-Hay, *The Quest for the Ark of the Covenant: The True History of the Tablets of Moses* (London and New York, 2005), p. 109.
12 On this encounter see Edward Ullendorff, 'The Confessio Fidei of King Claudius of Ethiopia', *Journal of Semitic Studies*, XXXII/1 (1987), pp. 159–76, and more generally Leonardo Cohen, *The Missionary Strategies of the Jesuits in Ethiopia (1555–1632)* (Wiesbaden, 2009); Andreu Martinez D'alos-Moner, *Envoys of a Human God: The Jesuit Mission in Ethiopia, 1557–1632* (Leiden, 2015).

13 Edward Ullendorff, 'Hebraic-Jewish Elements in Abyssinian (Monophysite) Christianity', *Journal of Semitic Studies*, I/3 (1956), pp. 216–56; Maxime Rodinson, 'Sur la question des "influences juives" en Éthiopie', *Journal of Semitic Studies*, IX/1 (1964), pp. 11–19; Maxime Rodinson, 'Review of Ullendorff 1960', *Bibliotheca Orientalis*, XXI (1964), pp. 238–45. All three of these have been reproduced, and in the case of Rodinson both are translated into English, in *Languages and Cultures of Eastern Christianity: Ethiopian*, ed. Alessandro Bausi (London, 2017), pp. 121–61 (Ullendorff) and pp. 163–78, 179–86 (Rodinson).

14 Marie-Laure Derat, 'The Zāgʷē Dynasty (11–13th centuries) and King Yemreḥanna Krestos', *Annales d'Éthiopie*, XXV/1 (2010), pp. 157–96. Maurice Halbwachs, *La topographie légendaire des Évangiles en Terre Sainte: Étude de mémoire collective* (Paris, 1941).

2 THE RISE OF AKSUM

1 Michael J. Harrower et al., 'Beta Samati: Discovery and Excavation of an Aksumite Town', *Antiquity*, XCIII/372 (2019), pp. 1534–52 (p. 1534).

2 See my 'Periodization of Ethiopian History: Reflections, Questions, and Some Modest Suggestions', *Aethiopica*, XXVII (forthcoming).

3 Pre-Aksumite 800–360 BCE; Proto-Aksumite 360–80 BCE; Early Aksumite 80 BCE–160 CE; Classic Aksumite 160–380 CE; Middle Aksumite 380–580 CE; Late Aksumite 580–825 CE; Post-Aksumite 825–900 CE. For this chronology see Kathryn Bard et al., 'The Chronology of Aksum (Tigrai, Ethiopia): A View from Bieta Giyorgis', *Azania: Archaeological Research in Africa*, XLIX/3 (2014), pp. 285–316.

4 Rainer Voigt, 'Aethiopia', in *Encyclopaedia Aethiopica*, vol. I, ed. Siegbert Uhlig (Wiesbaden, 2003), p. 163; Stuart Munro-Hay, 'Arabia', ibid., p. 295.

5 Rodolfo Fattovich, 'Reconsidering Yeha, *c*. 800–400 BC', *African Archaeological Review*, XXVI/4 (2009), pp. 275–90.

6 Daʿəmat or Daʿamat; the vocalization is unknown.

7 Sarah Japp et al., 'Yeha and Hawelti: Cultural Contacts between Sabaʾ and Dʿmt – New Research by the German Archaeological Institute in Ethiopia', *Proceedings of the Seminar for Arabian Studies*, XLI (2011), pp. 145–60; David W. Phillipson, 'Relations between Southern Arabia and the Northern Horn of Africa during the Last Millennium BC', *Proceedings of the Seminar for Arabian Studies*, XLI (2011), pp. 257–65.

8 For recent finds in eastern Təgray see Anne Benoist et al., 'What was the South Arabian Impact on the Development of Ethiopian Margins in Antiquity? Evolution of Settlement Patterns in the Wakarida Region from Pre-Aksumite to Late Aksumite Periods', in *South Arabian Long-Distance Trade in Antiquity 'Out of Arabia'*, ed. George Hatke and Ronald Ruzicka (Newcastle upon Tyne, 2021), pp. 111–53.

9 Alexandra Porter, 'Amphora Trade between South Arabia and East Africa in the First Millennium BC: A Re-Examination of the Evidence', *Proceedings of the Seminar for Arabian Studies*, XXXIV (2004), pp. 261–75.

10 Michael J. Harrower et al., 'Water, Geography, and Aksumite Civilization: The Southern Red Sea Archaeological Histories (SRSAH) Project Survey (2009–2016)', in *Spatial Approaches in African Archaeology*, ed. Cameron Gokee and Carla Klehm (Singapore, 2020), pp. 51–67; Catherine D'Andrea et al., 'The Pre-Aksumite and Aksumite Settlement of NE Tigrai, Ethiopia', *Journal of Field Archaeology*, XXXIII/2 (2008), pp. 151–76.

11 Sheila Boardman, 'The Agricultural Foundation of the Aksumite Empire, Ethiopia', in *The Exploitation of Plant Resources in Ancient Africa*, ed. Marijke van der Veen (New York, 1999), pp. 137–47.

12 I am grateful to the anonymous reader of this manuscript for their observation that 'In Harar, Christians eat ənğära from teff, while Muslim ənğära is invariably made from sorghum. The distinction enables the two communities to retain a social distance between each other.'

13 Catherine A. D'Andrea, 'T'ef (*Eragrostis tef*) in Ancient Agricultural Systems of Highland Ethiopia', *Economic Botany*, LXII/4 (2008), pp. 547–66; see Hiroki Ishikawa, 'Increase in Teff Consumption in Northern Ethiopia between the 16th and 18th Centuries and the Birth of Injera', *African Study Monographs: Supplementary Issue*, LXI (2023), pp. 7–40.

14 Tekle Hagos, 'The Choice of Aksum as a Metropolis', *Annales d'Éthiopie*, XXV/1 (2010), pp. 139–56.

15 Timothy Power, *The Red Sea from Byzantium to the Caliphate: AD 500–1000* (Oxford, 2012), p. 15.

16 Stuart Munro-Hay, *Aksum: An African Civilization of Late Antiquity* (Edinburgh, 1991), pp. 223, 227.

17 The claim that Adulis initially controlled the interior, including Aksum, and only later submitted to Aksumite authorities remains controversial. See François-Xavier Fauvelle, 'Les inscriptions d'Adoulis (Érythrée): Fragments d'un royaume d'influence hellénistique et gréco-romaine sur la côte africaine de la Mer rouge', *Bulletin de l'Institut français d'archéologie orientale*, CIX (2009), pp. 135–60.

18 David Peacock and Lucy Blue, *The Ancient Red Sea Port of Adulis, Eritrea: Report of the Eritro-British Expedition, 2004–5* (Oxford, 2007); Chiara Zazzaro, *The Ancient Red Sea Port of Adulis and the Eritrean Coastal Region: Previous Investigations and Museum Collections* (Cambridge, 2013).

19 Lionel Casson, *The Periplus Maris Erythraei: Text with Introduction, Translation, and Commentary* (Princeton, NJ, 1989); Eivind Heldaas Seland, 'The Periplus of the Erythraean Sea: A Network Approach', *Asian Review of World Histories*, IV/2 (2016), pp. 191–205.

20 Casson, *The Periplus*, p. 54.

21 George Hatke, 'The Aksumites in South Arabia: An African Diaspora of Late Antiquity', in *Migration Histories of the Medieval Afroeurasian Transition Zone: Aspects of Mobility between Africa, Asia and Europe, 300–1500 CE*, ed. Johannes Preiser-Kapeller, Lucian Reinfandt and Yannis Stouraitis (Leiden, 2020), pp. 297–305.

22 This is a name assigned to the anonymous author of the text. See Cosmas Indicopleustès, *Topographie chrétienne*, vol. I (books I–IV), ed. Wanda Wolska-Conus (Sources chrétiennes, no. 141) (Paris, 1968).

23 See Glen Warren Bowersock, *The Throne of Adulis: Red Sea Wars on the Eve of Islam* (Oxford, 2013), for his excellent discussion of this text and its milieu; quote at p. 48.

24 Nepheline syenite is a granite-like rock consisting of a quartz-free aluminium silicate primarily composed of the minerals nepheline, microcline and albite.

25 See Andrea Manzo, 'The Great Aksumite Decorated Stelae: Architectural Characteristics, Functions, and Meanings', *Aethiopica*, XXIII (2020), pp. 7–30; David W. Phillipson, 'The Significance and Symbolism of Aksumite Stelae', *Cambridge Archaeological Journal*, IV/2 (1994), pp. 189–210.

26 August Dillmann, *Lexicon Linguae Aethiopicae* (New York, 1955), p. 750.

27 Stuart Munro-Hay and Bent Juel-Jensen, *Aksumite Coinage* (London, 1995); Wolfgang R. O. Hahn in collaboration with Robert Keck, *Münzgeschichte der Aksumitenkönige in der Spätantike* (Vienna, 2020).

28 Aaron Michael Butts, 'Coins as a Source for History: The Case of the Aksumite Kingdom', in *Ethiopia at the Crossroads*, ed. Christine Sciacca, exh. cat., Walters Art Museum, Baltimore, MD (New Haven, CT, and London, 2024), p. 155.

3 A CHRISTIAN KINGDOM

1 Francisco Álvares, *The Prester John of the Indies: A True Relation of the Lands of the Prester John, Being the Narrative of the Portuguese Embassy to Ethiopia in 1520*, ed. Charles Fraser Beckingham and George Wynn Brereton Huntingford (Cambridge, 1961), pp. 148–51.

2 Marilyn E. Heldman, 'Creating Sacred Space: Orthodox Churches of the Ethiopian American Diaspora', in *Creating the Ethiopian Diaspora*, ed. Kay Kaufman Shelemay and Steven Kaplan (Los Angeles, CA, 2015), p. 105.

3 I use here with minor editorial changes the version found in Stuart Munro-Hay, *Aksum: An African Civilization of Late Antiquity* (Edinburgh, 1991), pp. 202–4.

4 For a valuable survey see Andrew Robinson's Lost Civilizations title *The Indus* (London, 2021).

5 Massimo Villa, 'Frumentius in the Ethiopic Sources: Mythopoeia and Text-Critical Considerations', *Rassegna di studi etiopici*, I/48 (2017), pp. 87–111.

6 Sazana(s) is mentioned as a co-ruler both in this letter and in an inscription commemorating one of 'Ezana's campaigns against the Beǧa. He was a military leader, who is referred to as the king's brother and may have become a co-ruler. This co-monarchy is also hinted at in later traditions which hold that the first rulers to accept Christianity were (Ǝllä) Abrəha and (Ǝllä) Aṣbəḥa, both of which are names that echo those of important figures of the sixth century.

7 In Ethiopic and South Arabian. In Greek he invokes Ares. See Aaron Butts, 'Ethiopic Christianity', in *Eastern Christianity: A Reader*, ed. J. Edward Walters (Grand Rapids, MI, 2021), pp. 382–3.

8 Ibid., pp. 383–4.

9 For a survey of these views see Steven Kaplan, 'Ezana's Conversion Reconsidered', *Journal of Religion in Africa*, XIII/2 (1982), pp. 101–9, esp. p. 103.

10 Francis Anfray, André Caquot and Pierre Nautin, 'Une nouvelle inscription grecque d'Ezana, roi d'Axoum', *Journal des savants*, IV/1 (1970), pp. 260–74.

11 See Butts, 'Ethiopic', pp. 382–6, for English translations of three (polytheistic, monotheistic and Christian) inscriptions.

12 Kaplan, 'Ezana's Conversion', but see also Paolo Marrassini, 'Lord of Heaven', *Rassegna di studi etiopici*, IV (2012), pp. 103–17.

13 Alessandro Bausi, Michael Harrower and Iona Dumitru, 'The Gəʿəz Inscriptions from Beta Samāʿti (Beta Samati)', *Bibliotheca Orientalis*, LXXVII/1–2 (2020), pp. 34–56.

14 Christian Julien Robin and Maria Gorea, 'Les vestiges antiques de la grotte de Hôq (Suqutra, Yémen) (note d'information)', *Comptes rendus des séances de l'Académie des inscriptions et belles-lettres*, CXLII/2 (2002), pp. 409–45.

15 Dibishada B. Garnayak, Manjil Hazarika and Kulbhushan Mishra, 'Cultural Interaction between Ancient Abyssinia and India: Archaeological Sources from 1st to 7th century CE', *Journal of Indian Ocean Archaeology*, X–XI (2014–15), pp. 133–46, esp. pp. 139–40.

16 For a history of this figure see Stuart Munro-Hay, *Ethiopia and Alexandria: The Metropolitan Episcopacy of Ethiopia* (Warsaw, 1997).

17 Ibid., p. 122.

18 Ibid., p. 161.

19 Ibid., p. 183.

20 Álvares, *The Prester John of the Indies*, p. 351.

21 See Marie-Laure Derat, *L'énigme d'une dynastie sainte et usurpatrice dans le royaume chrétien d'Éthiopie du XIe au XIIIe siècle* (Turnhout, 2018), pp. 87–146, where she argues for the Zagʷe period being crucial in this respect.

4 THE DEVELOPMENT OF THE CHURCH AND THE ARRIVAL OF ISLAM

1 Gabriele Castiglia, 'An Archaeology of Conversion? Evidence from Adulis for Early Christianity and Religious Transition in the Horn of Africa', *Antiquity*, XCVI/390 (2022), pp. 1555–73.

2 For a major research project re-examining the interconnections between Syrian and Ethiopian Christianity see Aaron Butts (principal investigator), BeInf – Beyond Influence: The Connected Histories of Ethiopic and Syriac Christianity, www.aai.uni-hamburg.de/beinf.html, accessed 6 May 2023.

3 Antonella Brita, *I racconti tradizionali sulla 'Seconda Cristianizzazione' dell'Etiopia: Il ciclo agiografico dei Nove Santi'* (Naples, 2010).

4 Antonella Brita, 'Nine Saints, in *Encyclopaedia Aethiopica*, vol. III (Wiesbaden, 2007), p. 1188.

5 Judith S. McKenzie and Francis Watson, *The Garima Gospels: Early Illuminated Gospel Books from Ethiopia* (Oxford, 2016). See also Jacques Mercier, *Art of Ethiopia: From the Origins to the Golden Century* (Paris, 2021), pp. 22–42.

6 Daniel Assefa et al., 'The Textual History of the Ethiopic Old Testament Project (THEOT): Goals and Initial Findings', *Textus*, XXIX/1 (2020), pp. 80–110.

7 Alessandro Bausi et al., 'The Aksumite Collection or Codex Σ (Sinodos of Qəfrəyā, MS C$_3$-IV-71/C$_3$-IV-73, Ethio-SPaRe UM-039): Codicological and Palaeographical Observations. With a Note on Material Analysis of Inks', *Comparative Oriental Manuscript Studies Bulletin*, VI/2 (2020), pp. 127–41.

8 Alessandro Bausi, '"Däbrä Dammo", Not "Däbrä Damo"', *Géolinguistique*, XX (2020), http://journals.openedition.org; Niall Finneran, 'Hermits, Saints, and Snakes: The Archaeology of the Early Ethiopian Monastery in Wider Context', *International Journal of African Historical Studies*, XLV/2 (2012), pp. 247–71.

9 I am grateful to the anonymous reader of this manuscript for first-hand comments on these reports.

10 Castiglia, 'An Archaeology of Conversion?'

11 There has been a fair amount of controversy regarding the date of these events. I have adopted the chronology suggested by Iwona Gajda, *Le royaume de Himyar à l'époque monothéiste: L'histoire de l'Arabie du Sud ancienne de la fin du IVe siècle de l'ère chrétienne jusqu'à l'avènement de l'Islam* (Paris, 2009). See Glen Bowersock, *The Throne of Adulis: Red Sea Wars on the Eve of Islam* (Oxford, 2014), pp. 92–133, and Christian J. Robin, 'Arabia and Ethiopia', in *The Oxford Handbook of Late Antiquity*, ed. Scott F. Johnson (Oxford, 2012), pp. 247–332, esp. pp. 283–92.

12 George Hatke, *Aksum and Nubia: Warfare, Commerce, and Political Fictions in Ancient Northeast Africa* (New York, 2013), online edition available at http://dlib.nyu.edu, accessed 4 July 2024.

13 Bowersock, *The Throne of Adulis*, p. 93.

14 Werner Daum, 'Ṣanʿāʾ: The Origins of Abrahah's Cathedral and the Great Mosque – A Water Sanctuary of the Old Arabian Religion', *Proceedings of the Seminar for Arabian Studies*, XLVIII (2018), pp. 67–74.

15 Lawrence I. Conrad, 'Abraha and Muhammad: Some Observations Apropos of Chronology and Literary Topoi in the Early Arabic Historical Tradition', *Bulletin of the School of Oriental and African Studies*, L/2 (1987), pp. 225–40.

16 Robin, 'Arabia and Ethiopia', pp. 287–8.

17 See Alessandro Gori, 'Islamic Cultural Traditions of Medieval Ethiopia and Eritrea', in *A Companion to Medieval Ethiopia and Eritrea*,

ed. Samantha Kelly (Leiden and Boston, MA, 2020), p. 147 n. 16. However, it should be noted that there is no clear evidence for a cult at the shrine of the *nağāšī* before the sixteenth century.

18 Hussein Ahmed, 'The Historiography of Islam in Ethiopia', *Journal of Islamic Studies*, III/1 (1992), pp. 15–46. For an important recent collection of studies see Alessandro Gori and Biancamaria Scarcia Amoretti, eds, *L'Islam in Etiopia: bilanci e prospettive* (Naples, 2010).

19 Here too, recent scholarship has challenged the traditional view of Yared and his period. Marilyn Heldman and Kay Kaufman Shelemay, 'Concerning Saint Yared', in *Studies in Ethiopian Languages, Literature, and History: Festschrift for Getatchew Haile Presented by His Friends and Colleagues*, ed. Adam C. McCollum (Wiesbaden, 2017), pp. 65–93.

20 For the most recent attempt to synthesize the discussions on this important question see Gianfrancesco Lusini, 'The Decline and Collapse of the Kingdom of Aksum (6th–7th CE): An Environmental Disaster or the End of a Political Process?', in *The End of Empires*, ed. Michael Gehler, Robert Rollinger and Philipp Strobl (Wiesbaden, 2022), pp. 321–36, where he argues for a culmination of political events as the cause for the decline. I am grateful to Professor Lusini for providing me with a copy of this article.

21 Abel Ruiz-Giralt et al., 'Human–Woodland Interactions during the Pre-Aksumite and Aksumite Periods in Northeastern Tigray, Ethiopia: Insights from the Wood Charcoal Analyses from Mezber and Ona Adi', *Vegetation History and Archaeobotany*, XXX/6 (2021), pp. 713–28.

22 Yohannes Gebre Selassie, 'Plague as a Possible Factor for the Decline and Collapse of the Aksumite Empire: A New Interpretation', *ITYOPIS – Northeast African Journal of Social Sciences and Humanities*, X (2011), pp. 36–61.

23 Julien Cooper, 'A Nomadic State? The "Blemmyean–Beja" Polity of the Ancient Eastern Desert', *Journal of African History*, LXI/3 (2020), pp. 383–407.

24 *The Martyrium of Arethae and His Companions in Nağran*, 27.19–22, quoted by Hatke, *Aksum and Nubia*, p. 159.

25 Susana Bortolotto, Nelly Cattaneo and Serena Massa, 'Seasonal Watercourses as a Source of Wealth and a Cause of Destruction: The Water Management in Adulis (Eritrea) in Antiquity and Today', *LARHYSS Journal*, XLVII (2021), pp. 25–38.

26 Enno Littmann, *Deutsche-Aksum Expedition*, vol. IV (Berlin, 1913), pp. 43–8 (Inscriptions 12–14).

27 Quoted in Marie-Laure Derat, 'Before the Solomonids: Crisis, Renaissance and the Emergence of the Zag^{w}e Dynasty (Seventh–Thirteenth Centuries)', in *A Companion*, ed. Kelly, p. 36.

28 Quoted in Stuart Munro-Hay, *Ethiopia and Alexandria: The Metropolitan Episcopacy of Ethiopia* (Warsaw, 1997), p. 133.

29 Knud Tage Andersen, 'The Queen of the Habasha in Ethiopian History, Tradition and Chronology', *Bulletin of the School of Oriental and African Studies*, XLIII/1 (2000), pp. 31–63.

30 Ayele Tarekegn, 'The Mortuary Practices of Aksumite Ethiopia with Particular Reference to the Gudit Stelae Field (GSF) Site', PhD thesis, University of Cambridge, 1998. Based on the several dozen stelae, as well as the pottery and glass found at the site, scholars believe this to have been a 'middle-class' cemetery from around the third century CE.
31 Berhe Hiluf, 'Preliminary Report on the Archaeological Excavation of Mäqabər Ga'əwa at Addi Akaweh (Tigrai, Ethiopia)', *Annales d'Éthiopie*, XXIV/1 (2009), pp. 15–31.
32 It has been identified with Aksum, Gondär, southern Təgray and Ankober (Amhara), and even merely derived from the Gə'əz term *kəbur* (glorious).
33 Ronnie Ellenblum, *The Collapse of the Eastern Mediterranean: Climate Change and the Decline of the East, 930–1072* (Cambridge, 2012).
34 Munro-Hay, *Ethiopia and Alexandria*, p. 158.
35 Patricia A. McAnany and N. Yoffee, eds, *Questioning Collapse: Human Resilience, Ecological Vulnerability, and the Aftermath of Empire* (Cambridge, 2009), pp. 1–17 (esp. pp. 5 and 10).

5 A LEGACY IN STONE: THE ZAG^{W}E DYNASTY

1 Indeed, a homily in honour of Lalibäla probably dates to the nineteenth or early twentieth century. Marie-Laure Derat, 'Autour de l'homélie en l'honneur du saint-roi Lalibala: Écritures hagiographiques, copies et milieux de production', *Oriens Christianus*, IX (2016), pp. 101–32.
2 Jules Perruchon, ed., *Vie de Lalibala, roi d'Éthiopie: Texte éthiopien publié d'après un manuscrit du Musée britannique et traduction française . . .* (Publications de l'École des lettres d'Alger. Bulletin de correspondance africaine, x) (Paris, 1892); Nafisa Valieva, 'The "Gadla Lālibalā Collection of Textual Units": Tradition and Documentation', doctoral thesis, University of Hamburg, 2021.
3 For useful presentations of the previous views of the history of the Zag^{w}e see Sergew Hable Selassie, *Ancient and Medieval Ethiopian History to 1270* (Addis Ababa, 1972), pp. 239–89; and Taddesse Tamrat, *Church and State in Ethiopia, 1270–1527* (Oxford, 1972), pp. 53–66; as well as Carlo Conti Rossini, *Storia d'Etiopia*, part I: *Dalle origini all'avvento della dinastia salomonide* (Milan, 1928), esp. pp. 300ff.
4 David W. Phillipson, 'From Yeha to Lalibela: An Essay in Cultural Continuity', *Journal of Ethiopian Studies*, XL/1–2 (2007), pp. 1–19.
5 Taddesse, *Church and State*, p. 47; Marie-Laure Derat, *L'énigme d'une dynastie sainte et usurpatrice dans le royaume chrétien d'Éthiopie du XIe au XIIIe siècle* (Turnhout, 2018). For a convenient summary of Derat's main arguments see Marie-Laure Derat, 'Before the Solomonids: Crises, Renaissance and the Emergence of the Zagwe Dynasty (Seventh–Thirteenth

Centuries)', in *A Companion to Medieval Ethiopia and Eritrea*, ed. Samantha Kelly (Leiden and Boston, MA, 2020), pp. 31–56.

6 Taddesse, *Church and State*, p. 55.

7 For the complex history and possible erasure of this place name see Marie-Laure Derat, 'Du Begʷenā au Lāstā: Centre et périphérie dans le royaume d'Éthiopie du XIIIe au XVIe siècle', *Annales d'Éthiopie*, XXV (2009), pp. 65–86.

8 Derat, *L'énigme*, pp. 49–50, 56–7.

9 Ibid., p. 38.

10 Ibid., pp. 87–145.

11 Not to be confused with the Shäwan monastery of Däbrä Libanos, originally known as Däbrä Asbo and founded by the thirteenth-century monastic leader Täklä Haymanot.

12 Derat, *L'énigme*, pp. 30–38, 261–71.

13 Mikael Muehlbauer, 'A Rock-Hewn Yəmrəḥannä Krəstos? An Investigation into Possible "Northern" Zagwe Churches near 'Addigrat, Təgray', *Aethiopica*, XXXIII (2020), pp. 31–56.

14 Derat, 'Before the Solomonids', p. 50. See Alessandro Bausi, 'The Enigma of a Medieval Ethiopian Dynasty of Usurpers', *Orientalistische Literaturzeitung*, CXIII/6 (2018), pp. 439–44.

15 Derat, 'Before the Solomonids', p. 51.

16 Derat, *L'énigme*, pp. 195–256.

17 Marie-Laure Derat et al., 'The Rock-Cut Churches of Lalibela and the Cave Church of Washa Mika'el: Troglodytism and the Christianisation of the Ethiopian Highlands', *Antiquity*, XLV/380 (2021), pp. 467–86.

18 Jacques Mercier, Claude Lepage and T. Bittar, *Lalibela: Wonder of Ethiopia: The Monolithic Churches and Their Treasures* (London, 2012); Georg Gerster, *Churches in Rock: Early Christian Art in Ethiopia* (London, 1970); Marilyn E. Heldman, 'Legends of Lalibäla: The Development of an Ethiopian Pilgrimage Site', *Res: Anthropology and Aesthetics*, XXVII (1995), pp. 25–38; Irmgard Bidder, *Lalibela: The Monolithic Churches of Ethiopia* (Cologne, 1958); David W. Phillipson, *Ancient Churches of Ethiopia* (New Haven, CT, 2012), pp. 123–82; Claire Bosc-Tiessé and Marie-Laure Derat, eds, *Lalibela, site rupestre chrétien d'Éthiopie* (Toulouse, 2019).

19 Claude Lepage, 'Un métropolite égyptien bâtisseur à Lalibäla (Éthiopie) entre 1205 et 1210', *Comptes rendus des séances de l'Académie des inscriptions et belles-lettres*, CXLVII/1 (2002), pp. 141–74.

20 Jacques Mercier, *Art of Ethiopia: From the Origins to the Golden Century* (Paris, 2021), p. 57. Mikael Muehlbauer, 'An African "Constantine" in the Twelfth Century: The Architecture of the Early Zagwe Dynasty and Egyptian Episcopal Authority', *Gesta*, LXII/2 (2023), pp. 133–43. I am grateful to the author for providing me with a copy of this recent paper.

21 Niall Finneran, *The Archaeology of Ethiopia* (London and New York, 2007), p. 345; Eva Balicka-Witakowska, 'The Wall-Paintings in the Church

of Mädhane Äläm near Lalibäla', *Africana Bulletin*, LII (2004), pp. 9–29; Mercier, *Art of Ethiopia*, p. 53, believes it to be 'the first monolithic church ever built' and that it was completed in 1204.

22 Mercier, *Art of Ethiopia*, p. 53.

23 Heldman, 'Legends', p. 488.

24 This Aksumite church is today identified as the church of the Four Creatures (Arbaʿətu Ənsəsa) after the beings mentioned in Ezekiel 1:12–20 and Revelation 4:6–9, 5:6–14, 6:1–8, 14:3, 15:7 and 19:4.

25 Michael Gervers, 'The Rehabilitation of the Zaguë Kings and the Building of the Däbrä Sina – Golgotha – Sellassie Complex in Lalibäla', *Africana Bulletin*, LI (2003), pp. 23–49; I regret that I on this issue was not able to consult Marie-Laure Derat, 'La tombe du roi Lālibalā, l'église de Golgotha et un Saint-Sépulcre éthiopien', in *Qedemt et les espaces funéraires de Lalibela (XIe–XXIe siècle): Vies et usages sépulcraux d'un site* (Toulouse, 2023), pp. 19–36.

26 Gerster, *Churches in Rock*, p. 103.

27 François-Xavier Fauvelle-Aymar et al., 'Rock-Cut Stratigraphy: Sequencing the Lalibela Churches', *Antiquity*, LXXXIV/326 (2010), pp. 1135–50; Lepage, 'Un métropolite'; Emmanuel Fritsch, 'The Churches of Lalibäla (Ethiopia): Witnesses of Liturgical Changes', *Bollettino della Badia Greca di Grottaferrata*, III/5 (2008), pp. 69–112.

28 Marie-Laure Derat, 'The Rock-Hewn Churches of Lalibela: Bridging Local and Global Christian Culture', in *Africa and Byzantium*, ed. Andrea Myers Achi (New Haven, CT, and London, 2023), p. 233, referencing Fauvelle-Aymar et al., 'Rock-Cut Stratigraphy'.

29 Phillipson, *Ancient Churches*.

30 Gervers, 'The Rehabilitation'.

31 Stuart Munro-Hay, *Ethiopia and Alexandria: The Metropolitan Episcopacy of Ethiopia* (Warsaw, 1997), p. 134.

32 Mikael Muehlbauer, *Bastions of the Cross: Medieval Rock-Cut Cruciform Churches of Tigray, Ethiopia* (Washington, DC, 2023).

33 Marie-Laure Derat et al., 'Māryām Nāzrēt (Ethiopia): The Twelfth-Century Transformations of an Aksumite Site in Connection with an Egyptian Christian Community', *Cahiers d'études africaines*, LX/239 (2020), pp. 473–508.

34 Ibid., and for an elaboration of this point, see Muehlbauer, 'An African "Constantine"'. Muehlbauer also suggests a similar process around this time in the establishment of a church dedicated to the sixth-century saint Abba Afṣe at Yeha, pp. 143–51.

35 See Derat, *L'Énigme*, pp. 40–46.

36 Despite the claims of Ephraim Isaac, *The Ethiopian Orthodox Täwahïdo Church* (Trenton, NJ, 2012), p. 41: 'The Coptic relationship with Ethiopia was indeed never secured until 1270.'

37 Ewa Balicka-Witakowska and Michael Gervers, 'The Church of Yəmrähạnnä Krəstos and Its Wall-Paintings: A Preliminary Report', *Africana Bulletin*, XL (2001), pp. 9–47.

38 Mat Immerzeel, 'Coptic–Ethiopian Artistic Interactions: The Issues of the Nursing Virgin and St George Slaying the Dragon', *Journal of the Canadian Society for Coptic Studies*, VIII (2016), pp. 95–118.

39 Mercier, *Art of Ethiopia*, p. 51. It is not clear here whether Mercier is referring to the manuscript found in the monastery of Däbrä Libanos of Ham (Eritrea), which is one of the oldest surviving illuminated Gospel manuscripts. Alessandro Bausi and his colleagues suggest that the 'Aksumite Collection' may have been copied during the Zagʷe period. Alessandro Bausi et al., 'The Aksumite Collection or Codex Σ (Sinodos of Qəfrəyā, MS C3-IV-71/C3-IV-73, Ethio-SPaRe UM-039): Codicological and Palaeographical Observations. With a Note on Material Analysis of Inks', *Comparative Oriental Manuscript Studies Bulletin*, VI (2020), pp. 127–71.

40 Getatchew Haile, 'Highlighting Ethiopian Traditional Literature', in *Silence Is Not Golden: An Anthology of Ethiopian Literature*, ed. Taddesse Adera and Ali Jimale Ahmed (London, 1995), pp. 39–59.

41 See particularly the caveats expressed by Alessandro Gori in his important essay on 'Islamic Cultural Traditions of Medieval Ethiopia and Eritrea', in *A Companion*, ed. Kelly, pp. 142–61 (esp. p. 144).

42 Julien Loiseau et al., 'Bilet and the Wider World: New Insights into the Archaeology of Islam in Tigray', *Antiquity*, XCV/380 (2021), pp. 508–29. I am grateful to Mikael Muehlbauer for drawing my attention to this important article.

43 For the ease with which Islamic materials can be overlooked because of an assumption of Christian dominance see Mikael Muehlbauer, 'From Stone to Dust: The Life of the Kufic-Inscribed Frieze of Wuqro Cherqos in Tigray, Ethiopia', *Muqarnas Online*, XXXVIII/1 (2021), pp. 1–34.

44 Amélie Chekroun and Bertrand Hirsch, 'The Sultanates of Medieval Ethiopia', in *A Companion*, ed. Kelly, pp. 86–112.

45 Anaïs Wion, 'Medieval Ethiopian Economies: Subsistence, Global Trade and the Administration of Wealth', in *A Companion*, ed. Kelly, pp. 395–424 (p. 415).

46 'Archaeologists in Ethiopia Uncover Ancient City in Harlaa', www.bbc.co.uk/news, 16 June 2017.

47 Timothy Insoll et al., 'Material Cosmopolitanism: The Entrepot of Harlaa as an Islamic Gateway to Eastern Ethiopia', *Antiquity*, XCV/380 (2021), pp. 487–507.

48 Timothy Insoll, 'First Footsteps in the Archaeology of Harar, Ethiopia', *Journal of Islamic Archaeology*, IV/2 (2017), pp. 189–215; Timothy Insoll and Ahmed Zekaria, 'The Mosques of Harar: An Archaeological and Historical Study', *Journal of Islamic Archaeology*, VI/1 (2019), pp. 81–107.

49 Stéphane Pradines, 'The Medieval Mosques of Nora: Islamic Architecture in Ethiopia', *Journal of Oriental and African Studies*, XXVI (2017), pp. 1–47 (p. 28).
50 Kirsten Collins and Bryan C. Keene, eds, *Balthazar: A Black African King in Medieval and Renaissance Art* (Los Angeles, CA, 2023).
51 Charles Fraser Beckingham, 'Boyle Memorial Lecture: The Quest for Prester John', *Bulletin of the John Rylands Library*, LXII/2 (1980), pp. 290–310.
52 Marco Giardini, 'The Quest for the Ethiopian Prester John and Its Eschatological Implications', *Medievalia*, XXII (2019), pp. 55–87.

6 A 'SOLOMONIC' 'RESTORATION'

1 Alessandro Bausi and Alain Desreumaux, 'Une ṭablītō syriaque orthodoxe en Érythrée datée de 1295/1296: Un témoin des "métropolites syriens"?', *Aethiopica*, XXIV (2021), pp. 233–44.
2 Serge A. Frantsouzoff, 'On the Dating of the Ethiopian Dynastic Treatise *Kəbrä Nägäśt*: New Evidence', *Scrinium*, XII (2016), pp. 20–24; this region may also be the provenance of *Zena Əskendər*, an early part of the sizeable Ethiopian corpus concerned with the royal model of Alexander the Great.
3 Adam Simmons, *Nubia, Ethiopia, and the Crusading World, 1095–1402* (London and New York, 2022), p. 22.
4 Francisco Álvares, *The Prester John of the Indies: A True Relation of the Lands of the Prester John, Being the Narrative of the Portuguese Embassy in 1502*, ed. Charles Fraser Beckingham and George Wynn Brereton Huntingford (Cambridge, 1961), p. 149.
5 Jules Perruchon, 'Histoire des guerres d'Amda Seyon, roi d'Éthiopie', *Journal asiatique*, ser. 8, XIV (1889), pp. 271–363, 381–493; George Wynn Brereton Huntingford, trans., *The Glorious Victories of Amda Seyon* (Oxford, 1965); Paolo Marrassini, ed. and trans., *Lo scetiro e la croce: La campagna di Amdä Seyon I contro l'Ifat (1332)* (Naples, 1993); Manfred Kropp, *Die siegreiche Feldzug des Königs, Amdä Seyon Muslims in Adal in Jahre 1332* (Leuven, 1995).
6 Bertrand Hirsch, 'Le récit des guerres du roi 'Amda Ṣeyon contre les sultanats islamiques, fiction épique du XVe siècle', *Médiévales: Langues, textes, histoire*, LXXIX (2020), pp. 91–116.
7 Ibn Faḍl Allāh al-ʿUmarī in his *Masālik al-abṣār fi mamālik al-amṣār* (Routes toward Insight into the Capital Empires). Quoted by Amélie Chekroun and Bertrand Hirsch, 'The Sultanates of Medieval Ethiopia', in *A Companion to Medieval Ethiopia and Eritrea*, ed. Samantha Kelly (Leiden and Boston, MA, 2020), pp. 99–100.
8 For an important survey of economic life in medieval Ethiopia see Anaïs Wion, 'Medieval Ethiopian Economies: Subsistences, Global Trade and the Administration of Wealth', in *A Companion*, ed. Kelly, pp. 395–424.
9 Qʷälls (below 1,800 metres/5,900 ft), *wäyna dägga* (1,800–2,400 metres/5,900–7,900 ft) and *dägga* (above 2,400 metres/7,900 ft).

10 Donald Crummey, 'Abyssinian Feudalism', *Past and Present*, LXXXIX (1980), pp. 115–38; and *Land and Society in the Christian Kingdom of Ethiopia: From the Thirteenth to the Twentieth Century* (Urbana, IL, 2000).

11 Kay Kaufman Shelemay, *Music, Ritual and Falasha History* (East Lansing, MI, 1986); James Quirin, *The Evolution of the Ethiopian Jews: A History of the Beta Israel (Falasha) to 1920* (Philadelphia, PA, 1992); Bar Kribus, *Ethiopian Jewish Ascetic Religious Communities: Built Environment and Way of Life of the Betä Ǝsraʾel* (Leeds, 2021).

12 See the important discussion in John D. Y. Peel, *The African Poor: A History* (Cambridge, 1987).

13 Steven Kaplan, *The Monastic Holy Man and the Christianization of Early Solomonic Ethiopia* (Wiesbaden, 1984); Gianfrancesco Lusini, 'The Ancient and Medieval History of Eritrean and Ethiopian Monasticism: An Outline', in *A Companion*, ed. Kelly, pp. 194–216.

14 Marie-Laure Derat, *Le domaine des rois éthiopienes (1270–1527): Espace, pouvoir et monachisme* (Paris, 2003), pp. 87–136.

15 Gianfrancesco Lusini, *Studi sul monachesimo eustaziano (secoli XIV–XV)* (Naples, 1993); Olivia Adankpo Labadie, *Moines, saints et hérétiques dans l'Éthiopie médiévale: Les disciples d'Ēwosṭātēwos et l'invention d'un mouvement monastique hétérodoxe (XIVe–milieu du XVe siècle)* (Rome, 2023).

16 See Kaufman Shelemay, *Music, Ritual and Falasha History*; Quirin, *The Evolution of the Ethiopian Jews*; and Kribus, *Ethiopian Jewish Ascetic Religious Communities*.

17 Taddesse Tamrat, 'Some Notes on the Fifteenth Century Stephanite "Heresy" in the Ethiopian Church', *Rassegna di studi etiopici*, XXII (1966), pp. 103–15; Getatchew Haile, 'The Cause of the Ǝsṭifanosites: A Fundamentalist Sect in the Church of Ethiopia', *Paideuma*, XXIX (1983), pp. 93–119; Pierluigi Piovanelli, 'Les Controverses théologiques sous le roi Zar'a Yāʿqob (1434–1468) et la mise en place du monophysisme éthiopien', in *La controverse religieuse et ses formes*, ed. Alain Le Boulluec (Paris, 1995), pp. 189–228; Denis Nosnitsin, 'New Branches of the Stephanite Monastic Network? Cases of Some Under-Explored Sites in East Tegray', in *Ecclesiastic Landscape of North Ethiopia. Proceedings of the International Workshop 'Ecclesiastic Landscape of North Ethiopia: History, Change and Cultural Heritage,' Hamburg* (Supplements to *Aethiopica* series, II), ed. Denis Nosnitsin (Wiesbaden, 2013), pp. 61–88.

18 Antonella Brita, 'Genres of Ethiopian–Eritrean Christian Literature with a Focus on Hagiography', in *A Companion*, ed. Kelly, p. 266.

19 Marilyn E. Heldman, 'An Ewostathian Style and the Gunda Gunde Style in Fifteenth-Century Ethiopian Manuscript Illumination', in *Proceedings of the First International Conference on the History of Ethiopian Art*, ed. Richard Pankhurst (London, 1989), pp. 5–14.

20 Kaplan, *Monastic Holy Man*, pp. 92–100.
21 Ibid., pp. 120–24.
22 See the previous chapter. It is interesting to note that Stanisław Chojnacki believed that this beast was transformed in Ethiopian art from a snake to a dragon in the fifteenth century: 'The Iconography of St George in Ethiopia: Part II: St George the Dragon-Killer', *Journal of Ethiopian Studies*, XI/2 (1973), pp. 51–92. See also Andrea Manzo, 'Snakes and Sacrifices: Tentative Insights into the Pre-Christian Ethiopian Religion', *Aethiopica*, XVII (2014), pp. 7–24.
23 For a very important discussion of these see François-Xavier Fauvelle, 'Of Conversion and Conversation: Followers of Local Religions in Medieval Ethiopia', in *A Companion*, ed. Kelly, pp. 113–41.
24 Ibid., pp. 124–41.
25 François-Xavier Fauvelle and Bertrand Poissonnier, 'The Shay Culture of Ethiopia (Tenth to Fourteenth Century AD): "Pagans" in the Time of Christians and Muslims', *African Archaeological Review*, XXXIII/1 (2016), pp. 61–74.
26 Fauvelle, 'Of Conversion', p. 135; Beley Alebachew, 'Megaliths, Landscapes and Society in the Central Highlands of Ethiopia: An Archaeological Research', doctoral thesis, University of Toulouse, 2020. Beatriz Marín-Aguilera and Laure Dussubieux, 'Embodying Ethiopia's Global Golden Age on the Muslim–Christian Frontier: The Allure of Glass Beads', *African Archaeological Review*, XL/2 (2023), pp. 317–33.
27 Birgitte Bøgh, 'Beyond Nock: From Adhesion to Conversion in the Mystery Cults', *History of Religions*, LIV/3 (2015), pp. 260–87.

7 IN THE NAME OF THE FATHER AND THE SON

1 For much of what follows see Steven Kaplan's 'Seeing Is Believing: The Power of Visual Culture in the Religious World of Aṣe Zär'a Ya'eqob of Ethiopia (1434–1468)', *Journal of Religion in Africa*, XXXII/4 (2002), pp. 403–21; 'Found in Translation: The Egyptian Impact on Ethiopian Christian Literature', in *Narrating the Nile: Politics, Identities, Cultures*, ed. Israel Gershoni and Meir Hatina (Boulder, CO, 2008), pp. 29–39; and 'The Christianisation of Time in Fifteenth-Century Ethiopia', in *Religious Conversion: History, Experience and Meaning*, ed. Ira Katznelson and Miri Rubin (London, 2016), pp. 81–98.
2 Kay Kaufman Shelemay, *Sing and Sing On: Sentinel Musicians and the Making of the Ethiopian American Diaspora* (Chicago, IL, 2022), p. 48. See the lengthy citation from the sixteenth century from Frank Harrison, *Time, Place and Music: An Anthology of Ethnomusicological Observation, c. 1550 to c. 1800* (Amsterdam, 1973), pp. 50–51.
3 Thomas Boylston, 'Food, Life, and Material Religion in Ethiopian Orthodox Christianity', in *A Companion to the Anthropology of Religion*, ed. Janice Boddy and Michael Lambek (London, 2013), pp. 255–73.

4 T. Vandevelde, ed., *Gifts and Interests* (Leuven, 2000).

5 Donald Crummey, *Land and Society in the Christian Kingdom of Ethiopia: From the Thirteenth to the Twentieth Century* (Urbana and Chicago, IL, 2000), p. 28. Note that the differences between the dates in this text and those used by Crummey are explained in Getatchew Haile, 'Documents of the History of Aśé Dawit, (1382–1413)', *Journal of Ethiopian Studies*, XVI (1982), pp. 25–35 and Steven Kaplan, 'Notes towards a History of Aṣe Dawit I (1382–1413)', *Aethiopica*, V (2002), pp. 71–88.

6 Marie-Laure Derat, *Le domaine des rois éthiopiens (1270–1527): Espace, pouvoir et monachisme* (Paris, 2003).

7 Getatchew Haile, 'The Letter of Archbishops Mika'el and Gäbrəʾel concerning the Observance of Saturday', *Journal of Semitic Studies*, XXVI/1 (1981), pp. 73–8.

8 Verena Krebs, *Medieval Ethiopian Kingship, Craft, and Diplomacy with Latin Europe* (Basingstoke, 2021), p. 188.

9 Marie-Laure Derat, 'Élaboration et diffusion du récit d'une victoire militaire: La bataille de Gomit, décembre 1445', *Oriens Christianus*, LXXXVI (2002), pp. 87–102.

10 Of course, since new miracles occurred this book can never be said to have truly been completed. The Princeton Ethiopian, Eritrean, and Egyptian Miracles of Mary (PEMM) digital humanities project is a comprehensive resource for the 1,000-plus miracle stories about the Virgin Mary in Ethiopia, Eritrea and Egypt, and preserved in Gəʿəz between 1300 and the present, https://pemm.princeton.edu/en-us, accessed 4 July 2024.

11 Amsalu Tefera, *The Ethiopian Homily on the Ark of the Covenant: Critical Edition and Annotated Translation of Dərsanä Ṣəyon* (Leiden and Boston, MA, 2015).

12 Emmanuel Fritsch, 'Turning Everyday to Aksum Ṣeyon Unaware: King Zar'a Yāʿeqob's Kehedata Sayṭān Identified in the First Prayer of the Day', *Annales d'Éthiopie*, XXXVIII/1 (2013), p. 363.

13 Ibid., p. 369.

14 Bertrand Hirsch and François-Xavier Fauvelle-Aymar, 'Aksum après Aksum: Royauté, archéologie et herméneutique chrétienne de Ménélik II (r. 1865–1913) à Zär'a Yaʿqob (r. 1434–1468)', *Annales d'Éthiopie*, XXVII/1 (2001), pp. 59–109.

15 Deresse Ayenachew, 'Territorial Expansion and Administrative Evolution under the "Solomonic" Dynasty', in *A Companion to Medieval Ethiopia and Eritrea*, ed. Samantha Kelly (Leiden and Boston, MA, 2020), pp. 80–82; see also ibid., p. 60. However, while Zär'a Yaʿqob elevated and championed Aksum, he also limited its territorial extents and power.

16 Claire Bosc-Tiessé, 'Christian Visual Culture in Medieval Ethiopia: Overview Trends and Issues', in *A Companion*, ed. Kelly, p. 356; see also

Jacopo Gnisci, 'A Contextual Reading of Ethiopian Crosses through Form and Ritual', *Aethiopica*, XXIII (2020), pp. 256–68.

17 Jacques Mercier, *Art of Ethiopia: From the Origins to the Golden Century* (Paris, 2021), pp. 43–4.

18 Steven Kaplan, 'Finding the True Cross: The Social–Political Dimensions of the Ethiopian *Mäsqäl* Festival', *Journal of Religion in Africa*, XXXVIII/4 (2008), pp. 447–65.

19 Another tradition claims that Aṣe Dawit received a piece of the True Cross through one of his missions abroad.

20 The finding of the True Cross is commemorated on two dates in the Ethiopian Orthodox calendar. I refer here to the elaboration of the celebration at the end of the rainy season.

21 Taddesse Tamrat, 'The Mateb', *Ethnological Society Bulletin*, IX (1959), pp. 38–42.

22 Francisco Álvares, *The Prester John of the Indies: A True Relation of the Lands of the Prester John, Being the Narrative of the Portuguese Embassy in 1502*, ed. Charles Fraser Beckingham and George Wynn Brereton Huntingford (Cambridge, 1961), p. 516.

23 Getatchew Haile, *The Mariology of Emperor Zār'a Ya'əqob* (Rome, 1992), pp. 170text=171translation.

24 Enrico Cerulli, *Storia della letturatura etiopica* (Milan, 1956, 1961, 1968, 2018).

25 Alessandro Bausi, 'Writing, Copying, Translating: Ethiopia as a Manuscript Culture', in *Studies in Manuscript Cultures*, vol. I: *Manuscript Cultures: Mapping the Field*, ed. Jörg Quenzer, Dmitry Bondarev and Jan-Ulrich Sobisch (Berlin, 2014), pp. 37–77.

26 Zeus Wellnhofer, 'Die arabisch-altäthiopische Übersetzungsliteratur im historischen Kontext des 13. und 14. Jahrhunderts', in *Multidisciplinary Views on the Horn of Africa: Festschrift in Honour of Rainer Voigt's 70th Birthday*, ed. Hatem Elliesie (Cologne, 2014), pp. 467–95.

27 Edward Ullendorff, *Ethiopia and the Bible* (London, 1968), p. 32.

28 Alessandro Bausi, 'Ethiopia and the Christian Ecumene: Cultural Transmission, Translation, and Reception', in *A Companion*, ed. Kelly, pp. 217–51, esp. p. 229.

29 Aaron Butts, 'Ethiopic Christianity, Syriac Contacts with', https://gedsh.bethmardutho.org, accessed 18 November 2024, examines the connected histories of Ethiopic and Syriac Christianity through a multidisciplinary approach that brings together methods traditionally disconnected, including art history, linguistics, manuscript studies, philology, textual studies and history.

30 See Reference 10 above.

31 Bausi, 'Ethiopia and the Christian Ecumene'.

32 Getatchew Haile, *The Different Collections of Nagś Hymns in Ethiopic Literature and Their Contributions* (Erlangen, 1983), discusses the three types of these hymns, including those written by Giyorgis.

33 James De Lorenzi, *Guardians of the Tradition: Historians and Historical Writing in Ethiopia and Eritrea* (Rochester, NY, 2015).

34 Antonella Brita, 'Genres of Ethiopian–Eritrean Christian Literature with a Focus on Hagiography', in *A Companion*, ed. Kelly, pp. 252–81.

35 Habtemichael Kidane, *Celebrating the Holy Saints: The Origin, Evolution, and Liturgical Use of the Mälkə'* (Piscataway, NJ, 2024).

36 Derese Ayenachew, 'Evolution and Organisation of the Çäwa Military Regiments in Medieval Ethiopia', *Annales d'Éthiopie*, XXIX/1 (2014), pp. 83–95; see Merid Wolde Aregay, 'Military Elites in Medieval Ethiopia', *Journal of Ethiopian Studies*, XXX/1 (1997), pp. 31–73.

37 Marie-Laure Derat, 'Du lexique aux talismans: Occurrences de la peste dans la Corne de l'Afrique du XIIIe au XVe siècle', *Afriques*, IX (2018).

38 Timothy Insoll, 'Archaeological Perspectives on Contacts between Cairo and Eastern Ethiopia in the 12th to 15th Centuries', *Journal of the Economic and Social History of the Orient*, LXVI/1–2 (2023), pp. 154–205; Amélie Chekroun, 'Harar as the Capital City of the Barr Sa'd ad-Dīn (First Half of the 16th Century): From Its Emergence to Its Fortification', *Annales d'Éthiopie*, XXXIV/1 (2022), pp. 23–44.

EPILOGUE

1 Taddesse Tamrat, 'Fifty Years of Decline: 1477–1527', *Church and State in Ethiopia, 1270–1527* (Oxford, 1972), pp. 268–96; see Harold Marcus, 'The Decline of the Solomonic Dynasty [from 1500] to 1796', in *A History of Ethiopia* (Los Angeles and Berkeley, CA, and London, 1994), pp. 30–47.

2 Verena Krebs, *Medieval Ethiopian Kingship, Craft and Diplomacy with Latin Europe* (London and New York, 2021), p. 142.

3 David Robinson, *Muslim Societies in African History* (Cambridge, 2004) and Nehemia Levtzion and Randall L. Pouwels, eds, *The History of Islam in Africa* (Athens, OH, 2000). During my early years as a graduate student and junior scholar I had the privilege of studying and working with Nehemia Levtzion (1935–2003). Although my interests (Ethiopia, Christianity and Judaism) and his (Islam, West Africa) were far apart, his contribution to my growth as a scholar was immeasurable.

4 Giancarlo Casale, *The Ottoman Age of Exploration* (Oxford, 2010); Bruce Masters, *The Arabs of the Ottoman Empire, 1516–1918: A Social and Cultural History* (Cambridge, 2013); Salih Özbaran, *Ottoman Expansion towards the Indian Ocean in the 16th Century* (Istanbul, 2009).

5 Edward Ullendorff, *The Ethiopians: An Introduction to Country and People*, 4th edn (London, 1973), p. 73.

6 Merid Wolde Aregay, 'Southern Ethiopia and the Christian Kingdom, 1508–1708, with Special Reference to the Galla Migrations and Their Consequences', PhD thesis, School of Oriental and African Studies,

University of London, 1971. Unfortunately, Merid's dissertation, unlike those of many of his fellow students at the University of London, has never been published.

7 Charles Fraser Beckingham and George Wynn Brereton Huntingford, eds, *Some Records of Ethiopia, 1593–1646: Being Extracts from the History of High Ethiopia or Abassia by Manoel de Almeida Together with Bahrey's History of the Galla* (London, 1954); Mohammed Hassen, *The Oromo of Ethiopia: A History, 1570–1860* (Cambridge, 1990); Mohammed Hassen, *The Oromo and the Christian Kingdom of Ethiopia: 1300–1700* (Woodbridge, 2015); Tesema Ta'a, *The Political Economy of an African Society in Transformation: The Case of Macca Oromo (Ethiopia)*, ed. Catherine Griefenow-Mewis (Wiesbaden, 2006); Amélie Chekroun and Bertrand Hirsch, 'The Muslim–Christian Wars and the Oromo Expansion: Transformations at the End of the Middle Ages (ca. 1500–ca. 1560)', in *A Companion to Medieval Ethiopia and Eritrea*, ed. Samantha Kelly (Leiden and Boston, MA, 2020), pp. 454–76.

8 Richard Reid, 'Past and Presentism: The "Precolonial" and the Foreshortening of African History', *Journal of African History*, LII/2 (2011), pp. 135–55.

9 Girma Beshah and Merid Wolde Aregay, *The Question of the Union of the Churches in Luso-Ethiopian Relations, 1500–1632* (Lisbon, 1964); Hervé Pennec, *Des jésuites au royaume du prêtre Jean (Éthiopie): stratégies, rencontres et tentatives d'implantation, 1495–1633* (Paris, 2003); Leonardo Cohen, *The Missionary Strategies of the Jesuits in Ethiopia (1555–1632)* (Wiesbaden, 2009); Francisco Álvares, *The Prester John of the Indies: A True Relation of the Lands of the Prester John, Being the Narrative of the Portuguese Embassy to Ethiopia in 1520*, ed. Charles Frazer Beckingham and George Wynn Brereton Huntingford (Cambridge, 1961); Isabel Boavida and Manuel João Ramos, eds, *The Indigenous and the Foreign in Christian Ethiopian Art: On Portuguese–Ethiopian Contacts in the 16th–17th Centuries* (London, 2017); Hervé Pennec, Isabel Boavida and Manuel João Ramos, eds, *Pedro Páez's History of Ethiopia, 1622*, vols I–II, trans. Christopher J. Tribe (London, 2011); Andreu Martínez d'Alòs-Moner, *Envoys of a Human God: The Jesuit Mission to Christian Ethiopia, 1557–1632* (Leiden and Boston, MA, 2015); Víctor M. Fernández et al., *The Archaeology of the Jesuit Missions in Ethiopia (1557–1632)* (Leiden and Boston, MA, 2017).

10 Ullendorff continued to publish new editions of *The Ethiopians* with only minor revisions for close to forty years!

11 Steven Kaplan, *The Beta Israel (Falasha) from Earliest Times to the Twentieth Century* (New York, 1992).

BIBLIOGRAPHY

GENERAL

The indispensable starting point for any understanding of the history and culture of Ethiopia, Eritrea and the Horn of Africa is the five-volume *Encyclopaedia Aethiopica* (Wiesbaden, 2003–14), edited by Siegbert Uhlig and Alessandro Bausi. This vast collaborative project is a landmark in the study of the region. Virtually every page of my book includes information gleaned from this source. Similarly, additional information about nearly every locale, person and literary work mentioned above can be found in its thousands of articles.

A recent one-volume overview of Ethiopia is Siegbert Uhlig et al., eds, *Ethiopia: History, Culture and Challenges* (Münster, 2017), which has also been published in German as *Äthiopien: Geschichte, Kultur, Herausforderungern* (Wiesbaden, 2018).

There are several scholarly journals dedicated to Ethiopia, Eritrea and the surrounding areas, including the *Journal of Ethiopian Studies* (Addis Ababa, 1963–); *Northeast African Studies* (East Lansing, MI, 1978–); *Annales d'Éthiopie* (Addis Ababa, 1955– [no publications 1990–2000]); *Rassegna di studi etiopici* (Naples, 1941–); *Aethiopica: International Journal of Ethiopian and Eritrean Studies* (Hamburg, Germany, 1998–); *International Journal of Ethiopian Studies* (Los Angeles, CA, 2004–); *Journal of Eritrean Studies* (Asmara, 2002–); *Journal of Oromo Studies* (Trenton, NJ, 1993–).

Since 1959 there has been the triannual International Conference of Ethiopian Studies. The most recent was the 21st, held in Addis Ababa in 2022, while the 22nd will be taking place September–October 2025. Proceedings are usually published: see Sushma Gupta and Taddesse Tamrat, 'The International Conference of Ethiopian Studies, 1959–1991', *Journal of Ethiopian Studies*, XXVII/1 (1994), pp. 29–142.

Professor Michael Gervers of the University of Toronto and Professor Ewa Balicka-Witakowska of Uppsala University have created *Mazgaba Se'elet*, https://ethiopia.utsc.utoronto.ca, an online database containing more than 65,000 photographs of Ethiopia (accessed 28 July 2024). See access instructions on https://dhn.utoronto.ca/project/mazgaba-seelet-treasury-of-ethiopian-images.

OXFORD BIBLIOGRAPHIES

Oxford Bibliographies online is an important reference source that offers readers advice on seeking out relevant works, including Marianne Bechhaus-Gerst, 'Northeastern African States, *c.* 1000 BCE–1800 CE', last modified 25 October 2012; Marianne Bechhaus-Gerst, 'Oromo', 25 October 2012; Claire Bosc-Tiessé, 'Art History of Ethiopia', 13 October 2021; Dan Connell, 'Eritrea', 28 February 2017; Alessandro Gori, 'Islam in Ethiopia and Eritrea', 24 July 2018; George M. La Rue, 'Indian Ocean and Middle Eastern Slave Trades', 25 October 2012; Andrew Mickleburgh, 'Horn of Africa and South Asia', 23 June 2021; Hagar Salamon and Steven Kaplan, 'Ethiopian Jews', 29 October 2013; and David H. Shinn, 'Ethiopia', 24 May 2018.

1 THE MANY FACES OF THE QUEEN OF SHEBA

For a valuable collection of articles which examine many of the issues raised in this chapter, including the date of the *Kəbrä Nägäśt* and the debate over Hebraic–Israelite influences, see Alessandro Bausi, ed., *Languages and Cultures of Eastern Christianity: Ethiopian* (London, 2017), pp. 121–86, 253–328. Afework Hailu, *Jewish Cultural Elements in the Ethiopian Orthodox Täwaḥədo Church* (Piscataway, NJ, 2020), attempts to place these elements in historical perspective. Unfortunately, it does not incorporate many of the historical revisions documented in recent scholarship.

Although it is still widely quoted, E.A.W. Budge's English translation *The Queen of Sheba and Her Only Son Menyelek; Being the History of the Departure of God and His Ark of the Covenant from Jerusalem to Ethiopia, and the Establishment of the Religion of the Hebrews and the Solomonic Line of Kings in That Country*, 1st edn (London and Boston, MA, 1922), is dated and not always accurate. Fortunately, Wendy Belcher and Michael Kleiner are preparing a new English translation. Other translations include Carl Bezold, *Kebra Nagast: Die Herrlichkeit der Könige . . . mit deutscher Übersetzung* (Abhandlungen der Bayerischen Akademie der Wissenschaften, XXIII) (Munich, 1905); Gerard Colin, *La gloire des rois (Kebra Nagast): Épopée nationale de l'Éthiopie* (Geneva, 2002); Robert Beylot, *La gloire des rois; ou, l'histoire de Salomon et de la reine de Saba* (Turnhout, 2008); Osvaldo Raineri, *Kebra Nagast. La gloria dei re. Salomone e la regina di Saba nell'epopea etiopica tra testo e pittura* (Rome, 2008).

2 THE RISE OF AKSUM

For many years the standard works on Aksum and Ethiopian history until 1270 were Carlo Conti Rossini, *Storia d'Etiopia*, part I: *Delle origini all'avvento della dinastia salomonide* (Milan, 1928) and Sergew Hable Selassie, *Ancient and Medieval Ethiopian History to 1270* (Addis Ababa, 1972). Among the more recent volumes are Stuart Munro-Hay, *Aksum: An African Civilization of Late Antiquity* (Edinburgh, 1991); David W. Phillipson, *Ancient Ethiopia: Aksum, Its Antecedents and Successors* (London, 1998); David W. Phillipson, *Foundations of an African Civilisation: Aksum and the Northern Horn, 1000 BC–AD 1300* (Cambridge, 2012); George Hatke, *Aksum and Nubia: Warfare, Commerce, and Political Fictions in Ancient Northeast Africa* (New York, 2013).

For a very important collection of the relevant inscriptions see Étienne Bernard, Abraham J. Drewes and Roger Schneider, *Recueil des inscriptions de l'Éthiopie des périodes pré-axoumite et axoumite*, vols I–III (Paris, 1991–2000). On coinage see Stuart Munro-Hay and Bent Juel-Jensen, *Aksumite Coinage* (London, 1995); a quarter of a century later Wolfgang R. O. Hahn, in collaboration with Robert Keck, published an updated examination of numismatics: *Münzgeschichte der Aksumitenkönige in der Spätantike* (Veröffentlichungen des Instituts für Numismatik und Geldgeschichte der Universität Wien, XXI) (Vienna, 2020).

3 A CHRISTIAN KINGDOM

See Alessandro Bausi, ed., *Languages and Cultures of Eastern Christianity: Ethiopian* (London, 2017), pp. 1–74. More generally, John Binns, *The Orthodox Church of Ethiopia: A History* (London, 2016), offers a survey of Church history by a non-specialist. Kirsten Stoffregen-Pedersen, *Les éthiopiens* (Turnhout, 1990), covers a wide variety of topics, including history, literature, art, ritual and theology. Ephraim Isaac, *The Ethiopian Orthodox Täwahïdo Church* (Trenton, NJ, 2012), is a very accessible collection of essays on a variety of topics. Although the bibliography includes much recent material, little of this appears to be integrated into the essays of the volume.

4 THE DEVELOPMENT OF THE CHURCH AND THE ARRIVAL OF ISLAM

On the issue of Syrian influences see, once again, Alessandro Bausi, ed., *Languages and Cultures of Eastern Christianity: Ethiopian* (London, 2017), pp. 187–252. On the early monks who are said to have led the 'second Christianization' see Antonella Brita, *I racconti tradizionali sulla 'Seconda Cristianizzazione' dell'Etiopia: Il ciclo agiografico dei Nove Santi* (Naples, 2010), which seriously challenges the historical value of these accounts.

The character of the monotheistic faiths in South Arabia prior to the rise of Islam has been the subject of considerable scholarship in the past decade. Sigrid Krogh Kjær, in an as yet unpublished dissertation, 'Monotheism, Kingship, and Religious Transformation in Late Antique Yemen: The Rise and Fall of Joseph dhu Nuwas', pp. 7–40, offers a very insightful survey of the relevant literature on the title's topics (www.utexas.edu). See also the earlier work Iwona Gajda, *Le Royaume de Himyar à l'époque monothéiste: L'histoire de l'Arabie du Sud ancienne de la fin du IVe siècle de l'ère chrétienne jusqu'à l'avènement de l'Islam* (Paris, 2009). Based upon her 1997 dissertation this volume offers detailed discussions of Ḥimyar from the introduction of monotheism until the conversion to Islam (pp. 35–167) and the relationship between state and society (pp. 171–252). Particularly relevant to Aksum is the suggested revision of the chronology of Himyarite rulers, including Ḏū Nuwās and Abraha.

Christian J. Robin, ed., *Le Judaïsme de l'Arabie antique: actes du Colloque de Jérusalem (Février 2006)* (Collection Judaïsme ancien et origines du christianisme, III) (Turnhout, 2015), represents a collection of papers first presented in Jerusalem in 2006. However, references have been significantly updated since those presentations. Robin himself contributes a massive book-length essay, 'Quel judaïsme en Arabie?', pp. 15–195, in this volume. Another more recent lengthy essay of his is 'The Judaism of the Ancient Kingdom of Ḥimyar in Arabia: A Discreet Conversion', in *Diversity and Rabbinization: Jewish Texts and Societies between 400 and 1000 CE*, ed. Gavin McDowell, Ron Naiweld and Daniel Stökl Ben Ezra (Cambridge, 2021), pp. 165–270.

On the Red Sea wars see Glen W. Bowersock, *The Throne of Adulis: Red Sea Wars on the Eve of Islam* (Oxford, 2013). A briefer account of much of the same material is found in his volume *Empires in Collision in Late Antiquity* (Waltham, MA, 2012).

5 A LEGACY IN STONE: THE ZAG^{W}E DYNASTY

Marie-Laure Derat, *L'énigme d'une dynastie sainte et usurpatrice dans le royaume chrétien d'Éthiopie du XIe au XIIIe siècle* (Turnhout, 2018), represents a major revision of the history of the Zag^{w}e, and hence a crucial rethinking of Ethiopian history more generally. It is arguably the most important work in Ethiopian history since Taddesse Tamrat's *Church and State in Ethiopia, 1270–1527* (Oxford, 1972). There have been many important works about the churches of this period. Among the most important books are Jacques Mercier and Claude Lepage, *Lalibela: Christian Art of Ethiopia. The Monolithic Churches and Their Treasures* (Addis Ababa, 2012); Claude Lepage and Jacques Mercier, *Lalibela, capitale de l'art monolithe d'Éthiopie* (Paris, 2013); and Mario di Salvo, *The Basilicas of Ethiopia: An Architectural History* (London and New York, 2017), esp. pp. 93–149. This book is a major contribution to the architecture of Ethiopian churches and particularly to the thesis that prior to the late fifteenth or early sixteenth century rectangular churches dominated in Ethiopia: David W. Phillipson, *Ancient Churches of Ethiopia: Fourth–Fourteenth Centuries* (New Haven, CT, and London, 2009), pp. 123–82. Here and in his many articles Phillipson emphasizes the continuity between medieval and ancient Ethiopia. See also the collection of articles published as 'Dossier – Lālibalā: Textes, objets, vestiges', *Annales d'Éthiopie*, XXV (2010), pp. 15–111.

There is a vast literature about the legendary figure of Prester John. For a valuable collection of sources in their original languages and translation see Keagan Brewer, *Prester John: The Legend and Its Sources* (London, 1991). Matteo Salvadore, *The African Prester John and the Birth of Ethiopian–European Relations, 1402–1555* (London and New York, 2017), presents an important analysis of fifteenth- and sixteenth-century relations between Europe and Ethiopia in the context of European and Ottoman expansion. See also J.M.T.

Dixon, 'The Prester John Legend and European Conceptions of Alterity before 1800', PhD thesis, University of Cambridge, 2020, which calls for a re-examination of the relationship between mythic geography and scientific knowledge.

For many years John Spencer Trimingham's *Islam in Ethiopia* (London, 1952) was the standard work and only general survey of Islam in Ethiopia and Eritrea. Joseph Cuoq, *L'Islam en Ethiopie: Des origines au XVIe siècle* (Paris, 1981), offers a useful discussion of the history of Islamic history but is not, despite the title, a discussion of the Ethiopian Christian Kingdom. François-Xavier Fauvelle-Aymar and Bertrand Hirsch, *Espaces musulmans de la Corne de l'Afrique au Moyen Âge* (Addis Ababa, 2011), was the first systematic examination of remains of the Islamic civilization of Ethiopia and Somaliland in three decades. Alessandro Gori, Adday Hernández and Irmeli Perho, eds, *Arabic Literature of Africa*, vol. IIIb: *The Writings of the Muslim Peoples of Northeastern Africa* (Leiden and Boston, MA, 2023), provides invaluable insight into the literary heritage of the various Muslim communities in the Horn of Africa. Their material culture is surveyed in Timothy Insoll, 'Ethiopia and the Horn of Africa', in *The Oxford Handbook of Islamic Archaeology*, ed. Bethany Walker, Timothy Insoll and Corisande Fenwick (Oxford, 2020), pp. 417–45. A special issue of *Northeast African Studies*, edited by Julien Loiseau, was devoted to 'Ethiopia and Nubia in Islamic Egypt: Connected Histories of Northeastern Africa', XIX/1 (2019), pp. 1–8. More recently, Amélie Chekroun has edited a special issue of *Revue des mondes musulmans et de la Méditerranée*, CLIII (2023): 'Ethiopian Islam: Connected Studies of Medieval Horn of Africa'.

6 A 'SOLOMONIC' 'RESTORATION'

Although it was published more than fifty years ago, Taddesse Tamrat's *Church and State in Ethiopia, 1270–1527* (Oxford, 1972) remains the starting point for any discussion of the period after the rise of Yəkunno Amlak. It lays out the basic chronology of royal expansion and the challenges faced by the successive rulers. The 2009 edition (Los Angeles), with introductions by Getatchew Haile and Donald Crummey, is particularly valuable. Similarly important is Marie-Laure Derat's *Le domaine des rois éthiopienes (1270–1527): Espace, pouvoir et monachisme* (Paris, 2003), which offers detailed analysis of the relevant primary sources along with astute discussions of the ways in which the Solomonic kings exercised and expressed their power. More recently, Samantha Kelly has gathered the best scholars of the period to produce *A Companion to Medieval Ethiopia and Eritrea* (Leiden and Boston, MA, 2020). The title of this collection does not do justice to its richness and many of the authors consider their subjects (politics, art, literature, manuscripts, Islam, monasticism and so on) in a far broader historical context. Moreover, its rich bibliography, which extends over more than eighty pages, includes virtually every important scholarly work about this period.

7 IN THE NAME OF THE FATHER AND THE SON

Claire Bosc-Tiessé, Art History of Ethiopia, www.oxfordbibliographies.com, 13 October 2021. Among the important studies and catalogues which have been published since then are Jacopo Gnisci, *Treasures of Ethiopia and Eritrea in the Bodleian Library, Oxford* (Oxford, 2019); Jacques Mercier, *Art of Ethiopia: From the Origins to the Golden Century* (Paris, 2021); Andrea Achi, ed., *Africa and Byzantium* (New York, 2023), catalogues a recent exhibition at the Metropolitan Museum of Art; Christian Sciacca, *Ethiopia at the Crossroads* (New Haven, CT, and London, 2024), is the product of a 2023–4 exhibition at the Walters Art Museum in Baltimore, MD. The publication of the last of these only appeared in April 2024 and thus could not be properly integrated into this book.

It has been more than 55 years since a book-length survey of Ethiopic (Gəʿəz) literature: Enrico Cerulli, *La letteratura etiopica, con un saggio sull'Oriente cristiano*, 3rd edn (Florence, 1968). Among its predecessors were John Mason Harden, *An Introduction to Ethiopic Christian Literature* (London, 1926); Ignazio Guidi, *Storia della letteratura etiopica* (Rome, 1932). More recent brief surveys include Aleksander Ferenc, 'Writing and Literature in Classical Ethiopic (Giiz)', in *Literatures in African Languages: Theoretical Issues and Sample Surveys*, ed. B. W. Andrzejewski, Stanisław Piłaszewicz and Witold Tyloch (Cambridge, 1985), pp. 253–300; Witold Witakowski, 'Coptic and Ethiopic Historical Writing', in *The Oxford History of Historical Writing*, vol. II: *400–1400*, ed. Sarah Foot and Chase F. Robinson (Oxford, 2011), pp. 138–54.

There is no question that the foremost scholar of Gəʿəz literature in the late twentieth and early twenty-first century was Dr Getatchew Haile. For a selected bibliography of his publications, see 'A Selected Bibliography of the Publications of Getatchew Haile', in *Studies in Ethiopian Languages, Literature, and History: Festschrift for Getatchew Haile Presented by His Friends and Colleagues*, ed. Adam Carter McCollum (Wiesbaden, 2017), pp. 609–19.

Aaron Butts is currently engaged in a research project, 'Beyond Influence (BeInf): The Connected Histories of Ethiopic and Syriac Christianity', which interrogates the connected histories of Ethiopic and Syriac Christianity through a multidisciplinary approach that brings together methods traditionally disconnected, including art history, linguistics, manuscript studies, philology, textual studies and history. See previously his article 'Ethiopic Christianity, Syriac contacts with', in *The Gorgias Encyclopedic Dictionary of the Syriac Heritage*, ed. Sebastian P. Brock et al. (Piscataway, NJ, 2011).

The Ethiopian diaspora, and more broadly Ethiopia's relations with the wider world, is a neglected topic which has finally begun to gather the attention it deserves. See Kay Kaufman Shelemay and Steven Kaplan, 'Introduction', *Diaspora: A Journal of Transnational Studies*, XV/2–3 (2006), pp. 191–213. For much of history most Ethiopians outside their homeland were victims of the slave trade; see Giulia Bonacci and Alexander Meckelburg, 'Slavery and the Slave Trade in Ethiopia and Eritrea', in *Oxford Research Encyclopedia of African History*, available at https://oxfordre.com/africanhistory, 31 January 2023.

In addition to her essay in the volume she edited (*A Companion to Medieval Ethiopia and Eritrea* (Leiden and Boston, MA, 2020)), Samantha Kelly has published a major work, *Translating Faith: Ethiopian Pilgrims in Renaissance Rome* (Cambridge, MA, 2024); Verena Krebs, *Medieval Ethiopian Kingship, Craft and Diplomacy* (New York, 2020), provides an important re-evaluation of the first Ethiopian embassies abroad; so too, the co-authored, with Yonatan Binyam, *Ethiopia and the World, 330–1500*, part of the Elements in the Global Middle East series (Cambridge, 2024). See also the abstracts from the conference 'Ethiopians Abroad in the Middle Ages', held in Rome on 23–26 March 2023, available at www.efrome.it.

ACKNOWLEDGEMENTS

This book marks the capstone of my almost fifty years of study and research on Ethiopia. It would be impossible to list all the individuals who assisted me on my path from a graduate student in my early twenties to a veteran scholar and finally retiree. Moreover, from the perspective of almost half a century, I am acutely aware of how scholarly opinion has changed during my lifetime because of new discoveries and theoretical re-evaluations. It must be stressed that this volume is intended as a synthesis of existing research rather than an original investigation based on my personal in-depth examination of newly discovered primary sources or archaeological discoveries. As I have tried to indicate in my notes and bibliography, in every page of this book I have stood on the 'shoulders of giants'. Doubtless specialists, including scholars of literature, historians, archaeologists, art historians and others, will find much to disagree with in this book. It is my sincerest hope that this book will be taken in the spirit in which it is intended – not as a final word, but as a mid-conversation intervention, which will provoke further discussion and debate.

For more than thirty years the Department of Comparative Religion and the Department of African Studies (and later Middle Eastern and Islamic Studies) provided me with an academic home at the Hebrew University of Jerusalem. The Faculty of Humanities supported me throughout my academic career and most recently through the Leo Polack fund, which provided funding for this project. Professor Kay Kaufman Shelemay read the entire manuscript, helped shape it through numerous conversations and for over four decades has gifted me with her friendship and support. Dr Georg Hatke and Dr Mikael Muehlbauer both shared their expertise on early periods in Ethiopian history through detailed comments on relevant chapters. An anonymous reader contacted by the publisher went above and beyond the usual duties of a referee offering insightful comments, incisive criticisms and catching numerous places where speed and carelessness detracted from the text. Dr Bar Kribus prepared the maps, which would not have been possible without his expertise. The Mäzgäbä Sə'əlet: Treasury of Ethiopian Images of the University of Toronto under the directorship of Professor Michael Gervers was an invaluable source of many of the images that illustrate the volume. Both he and the numerous scholars who deposited material in this collection have my gratitude. Of course, any errors, omissions or lapses of judgement remain my sole responsibility.

Michael Leaman of Reaktion Books showed remarkable patience and offered astute advice as I prepared this manuscript. Alex Ciobanu, the picture editor for Reaktion, guided me through the handling of images, which I had not previously dealt with in my earlier books. Amy Salter directed me carefully and deftly through the process of turning a rough and raw manuscript into a finished book. In sum, I have never been as patiently, skilfully and knowledgably assisted in my work on any previous publications as I have been in preparing this book for Reaktion!

As always, my wife, Albert Owens-Kaplan, showed admirable patience in waiting for the completion of this volume, and our (grand)sons, La'vonte and Asaph, showed bemused patience. Even from a distance my children Booshun (Shlomo) and Yona were an inspiration.

It is my sincerest hope that this short volume does justice to the recent progress in reconstructing the history and broadening our horizons of the Horn of Africa. By its very nature it is built on the achievements of countless scholars both past and present and intended as an invitation for further work by generations to come.

PHOTO ACKNOWLEDGEMENTS

The author and publishers wish to express their thanks to the sources listed below for illustrative material and/or permission to reproduce it. Some locations of artworks are also given below, in the interest of brevity:

From *Abhandlungen der Königlich Preussischen Akademie der Wissenschaften aus dem Jahre 1906* (Berlin, 1906), photo Smithsonian Libraries, Washington, DC: p. 53; Alamy Stock Photo: pp. 35 *left* (Photo 12), 35 *right* (Maximum Film), 81 (Hemis/Franck Guiziou), 129 (STOCKFOLIO®), 146 (Grant Rooney); Binghamton University Art Museum, NY (gift of Adriana Lalor in memory of Anna and Caesar Mascherin, Acc. no. 2013.2.12): pp. 38–9; Boston Public Library, Rare Books Department: p. 65; British Library, London (Add MS 5415 A, fols. 15v–16r): p. 117; photo courtesy Timothy Insoll: p. 113; Institute of Ethiopian Studies (IES), Addis Ababa University (MS 422, fol. 74r): p. 127; courtesy Bar Kribus: pp. 17, 25, 45, 94; Mäzgäbä Səəlat, University of Toronto: pp. 42 (photo Cheryl Chanter), 49 (photo Lenka Vrlíková), 54 (photo Cheryl Chanter), 63 (photo Mario Di Salvo), 66 (photo Michael Gervers), 72 (photo Ewa Balicka-Witakowska), 73 and 76 (photos Jan Tromp), 83 and 85 (photos Michael Gervers), 90 (photo Denis Nosnitsin), 95 (Church of Kidanä Mehrät, A.M. IV. 12394 and YK-020 (in the church register AM 12393), fol. 2v; photo Michael Gervers), 101, 104 and 110 (photos Michael Gervers), 128 (Däbrä Särabi, fol. 104r; photo Michael Gervers), 140 (photo Ewa Balicka-Witakowska), 141 (Institute of Ethiopian Studies (IES), Addis Ababa University; photo Stanislaw Chojnacki), 142 (Gəšän Maryam; photo Diana Spencer), 143 (photo Jan Tromp), 145, 147 and 148 (photos Michael Gervers), 149 (Abba Garima Monastery; photo Michael Gervers); The Metropolitan Museum of Art, New York: p. 105; from *Le monde illustré*, XXXI/1559 (12 February 1887): p. 112; photo courtesy Mikael Muehlbauer: p. 108; photo Bertrand Poissonnier, from François-Xavier Fauvelle and Bertrand Poissonnier, 'The Shay Culture of Ethiopia (Tenth to Fourteenth Century AD): "Pagans" in the Time of Christians and Muslims', *African Archaeological Review*, XXXIII/1 (March 2016), reproduced with permission: p. 133; photos Stéphane Pradines: pp. 114, 115; photo courtesy Kay K. Shelemay: p. 14; Shutterstock.com: pp. 41 (Dmitry Chulov), 48 *top* and *bottom* (Artush), 102 (Glen Berlin), 103 (Artush); courtesy Patrick Tiessé, Claire

Bosc-Tiessé and Marie-Laure Derat/Centre français des études éthiopiennes (CFEE), Addis Ababa – *Lalibela, Ethiopia: Plans and Site Topographic Map*, 2011: pp. 98–9; The Walters Art Museum, Baltimore, MD (MS W.850, fol. 2v): p. 150; Wellcome Collection, London: p. 55.

INDEX

Page numbers in *italics* refer to illustrations